George F. Root

The Forest Choir

A collection of vocal music for young people

George F. Root

The Forest Choir
A collection of vocal music for young people

ISBN/EAN: 9783337298562

Printed in Europe, USA, Canada, Australia, Japan

Cover: Foto ©Thomas Meinert / pixelio.de

More available books at **www.hansebooks.com**

THE

FOREST CHOIR:

A COLLECTION OF

VOCAL MUSIC FOR YOUNG PEOPLE;

EMBRACING

"OUR SONG BIRDS' SINGING SCHOOL,"

MUSIC FOR CONCERT, SCHOOL AND HOME,

AND

SONGS, HYMNS, ANTHEMS AND CHANTS, FOR WORSHIP.

BY

GEO. F. ROOT.

CHICAGO:

PUBLISHED BY ROOT & CADY, 67 WASHINGTON STREET.

NEW YORK: A. S. BARNES & CO., 111 & 113 WILLIAM ST.

1867.

"OUR SONG BIRDS'"
SINGING SCHOOL.

CHAPTER I.

The teacher asks the class to notice how many times he sings *la*. He then takes the pitch G and sings eight sounds about as fast as the pulse naturally beats.

After they have imitated him, he turns to the blank side of the blackboard and makes eight notes thus : ♩ ♩ ♩ ♩ ♩ ♩ ♩ ♩ and says, " These marks may stand for the sounds we have been singing; they are called quarter notes."

He then writes the word *la* under each note, and says. " Now look on the blackboard and sing these sounds again, and you will be singing by note."

The teacher now sings to the same eight sounds, with careful enunciation, pronunciation, and a pleasant tone, such words as the following, (the class singing each line after him.)

No. 1.

Now to sing, let all be ready,
Voices cheerful, firm and steady—
Do not stoop nor look about you,
For we would not sing without you.

Faces pleasant, bright and cheerful,
Not one scowling, sad, nor tearful ;
So let each some help be bringing
To the happy hour of singing.

These lines may be written on the blackboard under the notes, and may be sung again, if thought best.

Now is the time to begin to train and cultivate the voices and tastes of the class. First, and most important, by good examples. Second, by such simple directions as they will understand about position, taking the breath, opening the mouth, speaking distinctly. and singing with pleasant, rather than loud and strained voices. Third, by such selections of words and music as are adapted to their states mentally and musically.

The teacher now rubs off all the words from the blackboard, leaving only the notes, and then sings to the syllable *la*, the lessons on the board only making one sound, in place of the last two When the class have observed, and have done the same thing, and have named the new sound a HALF NOTE, and those they have been singing, QUARTER NOTES, the teacher rubs off the last two quarter notes, and puts a half note in their place, making the lesson stand thus: He then sings to it such lines as the following, (the class imitating each line.)

No. 2.

Come ye timid ones draw near,
There is nought to dread or fear;
Sweet let all our voices be,
Give the tones out clear and free.
Speak distinctly every word,
That the sounds may all be heard.

As before, it may be a good plan to write these words under the lesson, and have the class sing them again, this time attending more to such things of voice culture, position, breathing, speaking distinctly, etc., as they can understand.

The teacher now clears the blackboard again, and turning to the class, sings to the syllable *la*, quarter and half notes, in a different order, perhaps thus: After the class have imitated him, he writes the lesson on the board. After they have named the kind of notes, (he pointing,) the teacher sings to the lesson such words as

No. 3.

One and all, hear the call, 'tis the hour of meeting.
Now in place, all front face, give the teacher greeting.
All around, hear the sound, of the song we're singing.
Oh to you, pleasures true, may its tones be bringing.

Such lessons as the following may here be added. If the scholars have these books, it will not of course, be necessary to write the lessons on the board.

No. 4.

La, la,   la,   la,   Do   we   give   the   tones   out   right-ly?
Ha, ha,   ha,   ha,   Will you   an-swer   us   po-lite-ly?
Half, quar-ter, half, quar-ter, quar-ter, quar-ter, half note.
La, ha,   ha,   la,   ha,   the   quar-ter   is   the   laugh note.

No. 5.

O   the   hap-py spring time,   the spring time,   the spring time,
How   the   mer-ry   birds chime,   the birds chime,   the birds chime.

No. 6.

Ma-ry, Jen-nie, Su-sie, Liz-zie, Nel-lie, Lou and Fan-nie,
Kit-tie, Net-tie, Mat-tie, Lot-tie, and our lit-tle Au-nie.

Sal - lie, Ger - tie, Ka - tie, I - da, Flo - ra, Gra - cie, Car - rie,
Jo - sie, John - nie, Char - lie, Frank - ie, Wil - lie, Fred and Geor-gie,
Li - na, So - phy, Let - tie, E - va, Do - ra, Ad - die, Bel - la,
How - ard, Jes - sie, Cy - rus, Ly - man and his sis - ter El - la.

Such questions as the following will show how well the class understand what has been done, and also serve to keep them in mind of the important things of vocal training. *How many kinds of notes have we learned? What is the name of the longer note? The shorter? How much longer is a half note than a quarter note? How much shorter is a quarter note than a half note? Should you stoop while you are singing? Should you open your mouth so that the sound will be free and pleasant? Should you take a full breath when you have time enough, while singing, or only catch the breath a little? Should you speak the words distinctly, or indistinctly? Should you ever sing so loud or so high as to make the voice sound harsh or strained?*

CHAPTER II.

The teacher asks the class to notice whether he sings a half note or a quarter note. He sings a half note to "*la*," and asks which it is. He then takes a lower pitch, (say F,) and sings again a half note.

Which was that, a half or a quarter note? Yes, the same kind of note, or the same length of sound; but listen again. The teacher then gives two half notes, as before, of different pitches, but now being nearer together, are more easily compared. *Were these two half notes alike in all respects, or different in some?* Yes, we may have half notes or quarter notes different in *highness* or *lowness*, and highness or lowness in music is called PITCH.

The teacher now asks the class to notice whether he sings half notes or quarter notes. He then sings five, four, three, two and one, in the scale of C major in quarter notes to the syllable *la*. *Which did I sing, half notes or quarter notes? What is the highness or lowness of sounds called?* Notice now how many pitches I make. He sings the same again. *How many pitches?* Listen again, and then sing the same.

After practicing from five to one, a few times with quarter notes, it will be a good plan to try it with half notes, and then the five sounds, in the following order as to length. Quarter, quarter, quarter, quarter, half, and then, half, quarter, half, quarter, half, &c., the teacher giving each example, and the class imitating and repeating, until the work is well done in respect to length, pitch, position, breathing, distinctness, and giving out the tone.

How many different lengths of tones have we? What are the names of these two lengths? (half note and quarter note,) *How many different pitches have we?* Every pitch has a name, just as every length has. The first pitch we sang, or the highest of these five, is named G. All sing four quarter notes to the pitch G. The next lower pitch is named F; the next E; the next D, and the lowest C. If you go the other way—from the lowest to the highest, the names of the pitches are like the alphabet: C, D, E, F, G. Sing the pitches now as I ask for them, making a half note at each pitch to the syllable *la*, G, F, E, D, C, C, C, C, D, E, F, G, G, G, G, G, F, E, D, E, D, E, D, C, D, E, F, G, F, E, D, C. That we may not be obliged to sing *la* all the time, we will learn the syllables that are often used for these sounds. The teacher then sings from five to one, with the syllables *sol, fa, mi, re, do,* and the class imitate. Now sing the different pitches with these syllables as I give their names; sing half notes. *What syllable is used for the pitch whose name is G? What for the pitch F? E? D? C?* The teacher then names the pitches, (without skipping,) and the class sing.

This is the time to see that the syllables are pronounced well, (right vowel sounds,) and enunciated well (right emission of the consonants.)

CHAPTER III.

The teacher turns to the blackboard, and draws slowly a horizontal line, two or three feet long, sounding the pitch G in one sound, while drawing it, and says: This line may stand for the pitch, whose name is G. As many times as I touch this line you may sing quarter notes to the pitch G, syllable *sol*. Now I'll put quarter notes upon the line, and that will save me the trouble of touching it. The line then stands thus:

No. 7.

| Sing | the | pitch | of | G | to - | geth - | er, |
| In | this | pleas - | ant | sum - | mer | weath | er. |

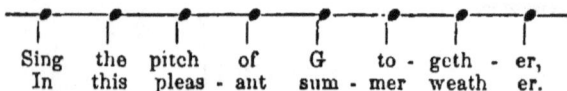

The teacher then clears off the blackboard and draws the line again for the pitch G, and under it another line, which he says may stand for the pitch F. thus:

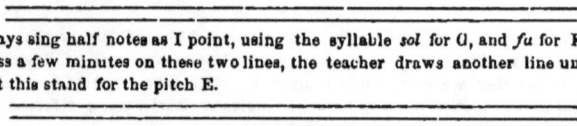

He then says sing half notes as I point, using the syllable *sol* for G, and *fa* for F. After exercising the class a few minutes on these two lines, the teacher draws another line under these two, and says: Let this stand for the pitch E.

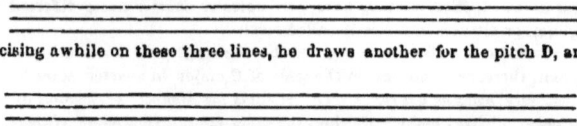

After exercising awhile on these three lines, he draws another for the pitch D, and exercises on the four.

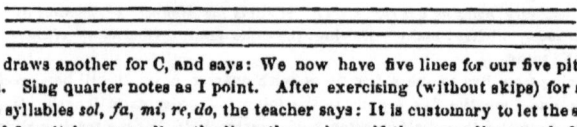

He finally draws another for C, and says: We now have five lines for our five pitches—one line for each pitch. Sing quarter notes as I point. After exercising (without skips) for a few minutes, and using the syllables *sol, fa, mi, re, do,* the teacher says: It is customary to let the spaces between the lines stand for pitches, as well as the lines themselves; if the upper line stands for the pitch G, the space next below it will stand for F. *What will stand for E? What for D? What for C?* Sing half notes while I point, according to this plan. After exercising a short time, the teacher says: These five lines, with the spaces between and above and below them, form what in music is called THE STAFF. The lines and spaces of the staff are named thus—(writing the names or speaking them while pointing :)

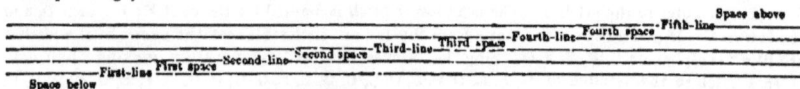

Space above
Fifth-line
Fourth space
Fourth-line
Third space
Third-line
Second space
Second-line
First space
First-line
Space below

Each line and space of the staff, and they are reckoned from the lowest upwards, is called a DEGREE. *How many degrees are there in this staff?* (Eleven.) *What is the first degree?* (Space below.) *The second? The third? &c.*

Our five pitches may be represented by any five degrees of the staff that we please to use. The teacher then writes such lessons as the following, (if the pupils have no books,) but is careful to have the class give the true pitches of G, F, E, D and C, whatever degrees of the staff may be used to represent them. *If we let the highest degree of the staff stand for the pitch G, what must stand for F?* (Fifth line.) *What for E? What for D? What for C? If we let the fifth line stand for G, what will stand for the other pitches?* It may be well for the teacher to exercise, beside questioning on different parts of the staff, but by no means change the pitch while doing so. Have the class always sing the G represented by the second line of the treble staff, whenever the five pitches are represented.

No. 8.

Sol, fa, mi, re, do, re, mi, fa, sol, fa, mi, re, do, do, do.

Clear -ly now, let all our voi - ces join and sing this ex - er - cise.

We will sing at morn and e - ven, Bird-like car - ols with the birds.
Here's the tune that has been giv - en—Let our glad hearts find the words.

The five pitches, G, F, E, D and C, and the two kinds of notes, quarter and half.

No. 9.

Sol, fa, mi, re, do, re, mi, fa, sol, fa, mi, re, do.

How beau - ti - ful the snow, On the sleep - ing earth be - low.
How light - ly does it rest, O'er the ear - ly called and blest.
How beau - ti ful the skies, Where the glad soul nev - er dies.

The same pitches, but in a different order, and represented by other degrees of the staff.

No. 10.

Sol, fa, mi, mi, re, do, re, mi, fa, sol, fa, mi, re, do.

Ug - ly crow, do you know? Here's a net that I've been weav - ing,
I shall lay it to - day On the corn, and stop your thiev - ing.
Sil - ly crow, you will know, When too late, that you're out - wit - ted,
Ev' - ry thief, comes to grief, And not one of them is pit - ied.

The same pitches, but represented by still other degrees of the staff.

No. 11.

Sol, fa, mi, re, do, re, mi, fa, sol, fa, mi, re, do.

Long - er, short - er, long - er, short - er, half and quar - ter notes.

Lit - tle Har - ry, do not tar - ry, Win - ter comes with joy.
Down hill fast - er, glad young mas - ter, You shall ride my boy.

The same pitches, but different tones, and different representations.

No. 12.

Sol, fa, mi, fa, mi, re, mi, fa, sol, fa, mi, re, do.

How the A, B, C is writ - ten, On this paint - ed card,
Now you dar ling lit - tle kit - ten, You must stud - y hard.
It would be a shame and pit - y, Just to run and play.
Do look on my lit - tle kit - ty Now, when I say A.

Keep the same pitches in both of these songs.

No- 13.

Sol, fa, mi, re, mi, fa, mi, re, do, re, mi, mi, re, re, do.

Mer - ry we go, the spring time is gay, the spring, the spring is gay.

Come to the fields and wood-lands a- way, To fields and woods a - way.
Come, for the birds and blos-soms are there; Are there this bright spring day.

No. 14.

Sol, fa, sol, fa, mi, re, mi, re, do, re, mi, re, do.

Come and lis - ten while I tell you in a sim - ple rhyme,
How we chil - dren sought the for - est, in the nut - ting time.
How the but - ter - nuts de - fied us from the top - most boughs;
They were then a lit - tle ver - dant; they are dry - ing now.

CHAPTER IV.

Although we may have our five pitches represented by any five degrees of the staff that are next to each other, it is common to have them represented in only two ways or places. In one, the fourth space stands for G, like No 10, and in the other, the second line. This we have not tried, but will do so now. *If the second line is made to stand for the pitch G, what will stand for F?* (First space.) *What for E! What for D?* Well, here we are at the lowest space of the staff, as we have heretofore represented it, but it may be enlarged by adding more degrees when they are wanted. We now want a degree below the space to represent the pitch of C, and we get it by adding a short line, thus:

After exercising a little while on this plan of representing the five pitches by pointing the teacher says: There is a character called the treble clef, which is always placed on the staff when the second line is to stand for G, and another called the base clef, which is always used when the fourth space is to stand for G.

No. 15.

Sol,   fa,   mi,   fa,   mi,   re,   do,   re,   mi,   fa,   mi,   re,   do.
Tre - ble clef, tre - ble clef,   C,   up - on   the   ad - ded line.
Lit - tle May, come and play, with   my pret - ty paint - ed sled,
I   will guide, you shall ride, till   the west -ern   sky   is   red.

No. 16.

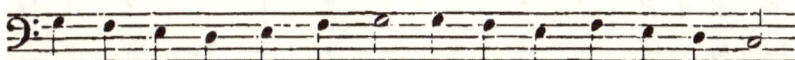

Sol,   fa,   mi,   re,   mi.   fa,   sol,   sol,   fa,   mi,   fa,   mi,   re,   do.
Space the fourth for base   clef   G,   and the sec - ond space for   C.
Line the fourth for let - ter   F, (mind this   is   no   tre - ble clef.)
And the let - ter   A   has place on   the fifth line and first space.
Line the third has let - ter   D; line the sec - ond stands for   B.
O'er the staff make care - ful search, let - ter   E   must have a   perch.

CHAPTER V.

The teacher says: Notice how many times I count one, two, &c. He then counts one, two, four times, making the counts even, and about as fast as quarter notes. *How many times did I count one, two?* (Four times.) All do the same. The time it takes to count each one, two, is, in music, called a MEASURE, meaning a measure or portion of time. Count again four measures, and while you are filling these measures or portions of time with counts, notice what I fill them with. (The teacher sings quarter notes at the pitch G, to the syllable *la*, while they count.) *In how many measures did you count, and I sing? How many notes did I sing in each measure? What kind of notes were they, half or quarter?* Now I will count while you sing quarter notes. The teacher then says: There are two kinds of spaces used in writing or printing music. The kind you already know, are those that are between the horizontal lines of the staff, and that stand for the pitches of sounds. The others are used to stand for measures, and are between perpendicular lines, thus: | | | | and these spaces are called measures, although they are not the real ones. *How many quarter notes did we sing in each measure? Then how many should I put in each of these spaces or signs of measures?* The lesson would then be written thus:

The perpendicular lines that divide the surface of the board into the spaces that stand for measures, are called BARS, and the two that are near together, to close with, make what is called a DOUBLE BAR. *How many measures are there here? How many bars?* Count four measures again. (The teacher now sings half notes, one in each measure, while they count, and then questions.) You may sing half notes while I count. I will always count one measure before you commence, that we may get a good idea of the time, and begin exactly together. After this is done, the teacher and class count and sing alternately, without losing the time, or stopping between the lessons. While the class count eight measures, the teacher sings a lesson, which the class immediately imitates, the teacher taking up the counting without stopping the regular movement, then when they get through singing, they strike into the counting again, and the teacher sings another lesson, or other words to the same. The following lessons will be good for this purpose. Alternate singing is very important, as there are many things of time, pitch, breathing, enunciation, pronunciation and style, that can be learned in no other way than by imitation.

No. 17.

La, lu, la, la, la, la, la, la, la, la, la, la.

See the trees, in the breeze, All their branch - es wav - ing,
Here the brook, ev - 'ry nook, Are its wat - ers lav - ing.

No. 18.

La, la, la, la, la, la, la, la, la, la, la, la,

Go win - ter, go win - ter, Come pleas - ant sum - mer time.

Oh ! bow - ers, glad bow - ers, When will your ten - drils climb,
Oh ! flow - ers, bright flow - ers, When will your sweet bells chime.

No. 19.

Sol, sol, sol, fa, fa, fa, mi, mi, re, do, do.

Ma - ry Ann, Ma - ry Ann, Where are you go - ing?
O'er the hill to the mill - brook bright - ly flow - ing,
There's the boat, just a - float. Shall we go row - ing?

No. 20.

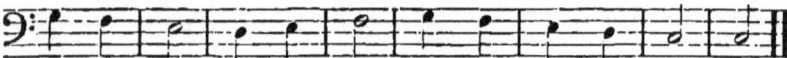

Sol, fa, mi, re, mi, fa, sol, fa, mi re, do, do.

Let me see, let you see, What was I then say - ing,
(Tho'ts that roam, hur - ry home ! You are sad - ly stray - ing.)
Oh 'tu - - this; if we miss at our re - ci - ta - tions,
; bo, cer - tain - ly dropped to low - er sta - tions.

CHAPTER VI.

The teacher sings G again, and then A to the syllable *la*. After the class have imitated, he tells them that the name of the new pitch is *A*, and that the syllable *la* is often used in singing it.

Sing quarter notes to the pitches I call for, using the syllables *sol, la*, &c. G, A, G, A, G, F, E, D, C, D, E, F, G, G, G. *What degree of the staff represents the pitch G when the treble clef is used?* *If the second line of the staff is used to represent the pitch G, what would properly represent the new pitch A?* (Second space.) *What represents the pitch G when the base clef is used?* *If the fourth space stands for G, what would stand for A?* *How many pitches have we now?*

No. 21.

| Sol, | la, | sol, | fa, | mi. | fa, | · sol, | sol, | la, | sol, | fa, | mi, | re, | do. |

Sing -ing   on   the   tree -top   high,   Who has home so blest as   I?
Lit - tle   nest-lings chirp to   me;   And my mate sings chee, chee, chee.

No. 22.

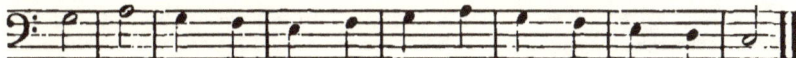

| Sol | la | sol, | fa, | mi, | fa, | sol, | la, | sol, | fa, | mi, | re, | do. |

Oh !   ho ! how   we   go,   From fast   to   slow, from high   to   low.
Oh !   ho ! life barques go,   From fast   to   slow, from high   to   low.

The teacher now sings G, A and B, in half notes to the syllable *la*. After the class have done the same, he gives them the names of the new pitch, and the syllable *si*, and exercises them a few minutes by calling, perhaps as follows: G, A, B, A, G, A, B, A, G, F, E, D, C, the class singing half or quarter notes as he may direct. *How many pitches have we now?*

The teacher then gives out G, A and B, in half notes, to the syllable *la*, and asks if B is a good pitch to stop on. If they do not perceive that another pitch is wanted to make completeness, the teacher begins at the lower pitch C, and goes up in half notes, stopping again on B. It is probable that all will then feel the want of another pitch, and at the teacher's direction, will give it readily. *How many pitches have we now?* (Eight.) *What is the name of the lower one?* (C.) Name these pitches from the lowest up to B. Listen while I sing the new pitch again, (to syllable *la*,) Now listen to the lowest pitch. All sing the lowest pitch while I sing the highest. One-half of the class listen while the other half and I sing these two pitches. Now the other half listen. (The teacher divides the class as it may be convenient.) You perceive what a singular agreement there is between these two pitches. (The teacher may make it more apparent, if he thinks best, by singing B, or A, or G, while the class sing C, and then again the lowest and highest pitch.) Partly on account of this agreement these two pitches have the same name C. We will, for the present, call them the lower C and the upper C. They have, also, the same syllable, *do*. It is said to be an octave, from one C to the next.

Let us now sing from the lower C to the upper, and then from the upper to the lower, making use of the syllables, *do, re, mi,* &c., attending to length, position, pitch, breathing, enunciation, pronunciation, and everything that will make our singing sound well. After this is done, the teacher sings to the syllable *la*, as follows:

No. 23.

Sol,   la,   si,   la,   sol,   fa.

And says : *Is this a good stopping or resting place?* He then sings the same, but adds E, and asks if that will do for a stopping place. After the answer, which will probably be in the negative, he sings the same, but now with the addition of E and D. After the questioning about D for a stopping place, he sings the same again, and after holding them a little in suspense on D, says you may all give the pitch that will make a good stopping or resting place, a home. They all give C. The whole lesson will be thus :

No. 24.

Sol,   la,   si,   la,   sol,   fa,   mi,   re,   do.

And the teacher says : The pitch that is the best to stop on, is called the KEY NOTE. *Which of all the pitches is the key note?* Let us see if the upper C is a good key note also. He then sings first to high A, in a lesson like the following, and questions as before :

No. 25.

Sol,   fa,   mi,   re,   mi,   fa,   sol,   la,   si,   do.

After stopping on B, and letting the class finish by giving C, the teacher says : You see that this upper C does very well for a key note, although, perhaps, not quite so satisfactory as the lower.

All sing from the lower key note to the upper, with the syllables, *do, re, mi,* &c. Such a succession of eight pitches, including the two key notes, is called in music a SCALE. Sing the scale ascending and descending in quarter notes.

No. 26.

Do,   re   mi,   fa,   sol,   la,   si,   do,   do,   si,   la,   sol,   fa,   mi,   re,   do.

O   come and sing the scale with me, Don't let our voi- ces dis - a - gree.
Now sing a - gain right mer -ri - ly, How pass -ing sweet is har - mo - ny.

We sometimes find it convenient to name the sounds of a scale by some of the names of numbers. The lower key note is called ONE; the tone next above it TWO, and so on up to EIGHT. *What is the pitch of one? Two? Three?* &c. As I give you the names, you may give me the sounds that they call for, to the syllables, *do, re, mi,* &c.

One, two, three, four, five, five, five, five, six, six, seven, seven, eight, eight, eight, eight, eight, seven, six, six, five, five, four, four, four, three, three, two, two, one.

The letter names we will call PITCH NAMES, and the number names, SCALE NAMES.

Scale names,	One,	two,	three,	four,	five,	six,	seven,	eight.
Pitch names,	C,	D,	E,	F,	G,	A,	B,	C.
Syllables.	Do,	re,	mi,	fa,	sol,	la,	si,	do.

In the following lessons, it will be well before singing each one, to question thus: *Which clef is here used? Which degree of the staff stands for the pitch G? Which degree then for the lower key note? Which for the upper? How many measures are in the lesson? How many bars, counting the double bar as one? What occupies the first measure?* (half or quarter notes) *What the second?* (and so on all through.) *What is the pitch name of the first tone? Second?* &c. *What the scale name of the first? Second?* &c. It would be well also, occasionally, to ask such questions as these: *What position shall we take, whether we sit or stand, while we sing? Shall we take a full breath, or but little? Shall we make the voices sound pleasant or harsh? Shall we speak carefully and distinctly, or indistinctly?* &c. Sing first with *la,* then with syllables, *do, re, mi,* &c., and at last with the words.

No. 27.

| Do, | do, | re, | re, | mi, | fa, | sol, | la, | sol, | la, | si, | do, | do. |

1. Where is lit - tle Su - sie gone? See what I have brought her,
2. She is at the riv - er side, Play - ing pranks with Ro - ver,

| Do, | do, | si, | si, | la, | la, | sol, | sol, | fa, | mi, | re, | do. | do. |

Sweet - est blos-soms from the lawn. Lil - ies from the wa - ter,
See a - round his neck she's tied, Wreaths of pur - ple clo - ver.

No. 28.

Do,   do,   si,   si,   la,   la,   sol,   fa,   mi,   re,   do,   re,   re.
1. She who gives the wrink-led frown, For the smile and dim - ple.
2. Life hath man - y thorn - y ways, Ere we reach the riv - er,

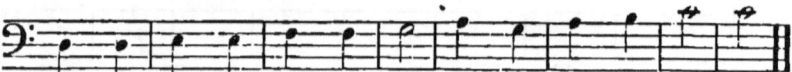

Re,   re,   mi,   mi,   fa,   fa,   sol,   la,   sol,   la,   si,   do,   do.
Lays her bright at - trac-tions down, And is worse than sim - ple.
Smiles will light the tang - led maze, Sun - light blest for - ev - er.

No. 29.

Do.   re,   mi,   mi,   fa,   sol,   la,   sol,   fa,   mi,   re,   mi,   fa.
1. Come with me,   ev - ery one, And you'll find we'll have some fun,
2. In the pond throw some sticks, Dogs are fond of all such tricks.

Mi,   fa,   sol,   la,   si,   do,   si,   la,   sol,   fa,   mi,   re,   do.
Car - lo there! come a - way! You're a rare dog at our play.
"Get it, sir!" it is done! Car - lo, too, en - joys our fun.

No. 30.

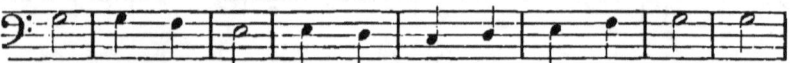

.Sol,   sol,   fa,   mi,   mi,   re,   do,   re,   mi,   fa,   sol,   sol.
1. Where? tell me where is Ce - leste, what shall I give her?
2. If thou shalt give all the heart's af - fec-tions ev - er;

La,   la,   sol,   fa,   fa,   sol,   la,   la,   si,   si,   do,   do.
There o - ver there, in a house be - side the riv - er.
No pow'r on earth shall your lov - ing spir - its sev - er.

CHAPTER VII.

All sing four quarter notes to the pitch of G, and try to have them neither loud nor soft, but medium in strength or power. Now again, but sing them loud—not very loud, but somewhat stronger than medium. Now medium again. Now soft—not very soft, but less than medium in strength.

In the science of music when they wish us to sing medium sounds they say MEZZO, (pronounced *metzo*,) or write the letter *M* (which stands for mezzo) over the note or line.

Instead of loud, they use the word FORTE, or the letter *F*. Instead of soft, the word PIANO, or the letter *P*.

Now sing a half note to the pitch G each time I call. *Mezzo, forte, mezzo, piano, mezzo, piano, forte, piano, mezzo, &c.*

No. 31.

Do, do, do, do, do, do, do, do, re, mi, fa sol, sol,
1. When you see the let - ter M, Mez - zo you must sing, sir,
2. Then a glad, he - ro - ic strain, For our coun - try chant, sir,

sol, sol, sol, sol, sol, sol, sol, sol, sol, la, si, do, do.
But when F is writ - ten down, Make the mu - sic ring, sir.
Let the wel - kin ring a - gain, At the name of Grant, sir.

No. 32.

Do, do, re, mi, mi, re, mi, fa, sol, la, sol, fa, mi, re,
1. Soft - ly sing, soft - ly sing, Let the tones be sweet and low; When-
2. Sweet and low, sweet and low, As the whis-per of the blest; When

Do, do, re, re, mi, mi, re, mi, fa, sol, fa, mi, re, do.
e'er you see the let - ter P, For it means sing soft, you know.
near to us the dear ones are, And the heart is hush'd to rest.

No. 33.

Do, re, mi, fa, sol, la. sol, sol, fa sol, la, si, do, do.
Mez - zo, for - te and pi - an - o, me - dium, loud and gen - tle;
Give them out in or - der fair, with-out a frown or wrin - kle.

The teacher sings a half and quarter note, making them alike in pitch and power. *How many sounds did I sing ? Were they alike or different ? Did they differ in length, pitch, or power ? What is the first length called ?* (Half note.) *The second ?*

The teacher now sings the pitches G and F, making them alike in length and power. *Did these sounds differ in length, pitch, or power ? What is the name of the first pitch ? The second ?*

The teacher now sings two sounds, one loud and tho other soft, but making them alike in length and pitch. *Did these sounds differ in length, pitch, or power ? What is the name of the first power ? The second ? How many lengths of sounds have we learned ? What are their names ? How many pitches of sounds have we learned ?* Name them, beginning at the lowest. *How many powers of sounds have we learned ? What are their names ?*

Can you make a musical sound without any length ? Do you suppose that you can make one without any pitch ? Can you make one without any power ? No; every tone must have some length, some pitch, and some power; but we may attend especially to one thing at a time—that is, we may keep the same pitch, and same power, and practice a good many different lengths; or we may keep the same length, and same power, and practice different pitches ; or the same length, and same pitch, and practice different degrees of power, as we have done, or we may continue them all together, and in the same piece havo differences of pitch, and differences of power, as we have also done.

What is that department in mathematics called in which you study about adding numbers together ? What is it where you study about taking one number from another ? Well, it is just on that principle in music. When we are studying especially about the length of sounds, we are in a department called RHYTHMICS. When we are studying about the pitch of sounds, we are in a department called MELODICS. When we are studying about the power of sounds, we are in a department called DYNAMICS. *What is the name of the department in music that treats of the length of sounds ? What is the name of the department that treats of the pitch of sounds ? What that treats of the power of sounds ?* Yes, and Rhythmics, Melodics, and Dynamics include everything of this subject. When you know all about these three departments, you will know all that can be known of music.

Are notes rhythmic, melodic, or dynamic characters ? Is the staff a rhythmic, melodic, or dynamic character ? How about clefs, bars, &c., &c.

When no dynamic mark is given, mezzo is always understood.

No. 34.

Sol, sol, sol, sol, sol, sol, la, sol, fa, mi, re, mi.
1. Oh, lis - ten! *do* list— the bird up - on the high - est
2. Rhyth - mics, yes, Rhyth - mics and Mo - lod - ics, and Mo - lod-

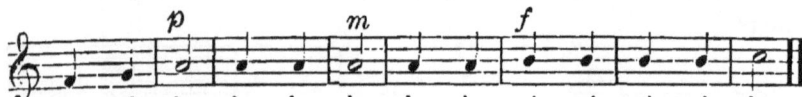

p   *m*   *f*

Fa, sol, la, la, la, la, la, la, si, si, si, si, do,
bough sings chee, chee—sings chee, chee, is sing - ing un - to me.
ics, then Dy - nam - ics, Dy - nam - ics, last of all the three.

CHAPTER VIII.

The teacher says: Count four measures of time, but instead of saying one, two, in each measure, say one, two, three; that will make the measures a little longer. Count evenly and steadily, letting the voice drop at the last count of each measure.

Now I'll count and you sing quarter notes to the pitch of G. That would be represented thus·

No. 35.

La, la, la, la, la, la, la, la, la, la, la, la.
Cheer - ful - ly, Care - ful - ly, Hope - ful - ly, Joy - ful - ly.

Measures that have three parts are called TRIPLE MEASURES; those that we have been practicing are called DOUBLE MEASURES.

Sing four triple measures, putting a half and quarter note in thus:

No. 36.

La, la, la, la, la, la, la, la.
O how long the way we're go - ing.

Now each measure again, filling each measure with a single sound. This is a new length, and is named DOTTED HALF NOTE. It is represented thus: No. 37.

How slow, we go.

To which department does the new measure and the new note belong, Rhythmics, Melodics, or Dynamics? Before singing the following lessons, question about the measure, the kind of notes, clef, pitch names, scale names; and if necessary, remind the class about position, breathing, giving out the tone, enunciation, and pronunciation.

No. 38.

m   *f*

Do, do, do, re, re, re, mi, mi, mi, fa, sol, sol, sol.
1. Now let the tones of the new meas - ure ring, For you will
2. Un - writ - ten meas-ures much sweet - er can be, Songs of tho

m   *p*

La, la. la, si, si, si, do, do, si, la, sol, fa, mi, re, do.
find it a ver - y good thing; ver - y good thing; ver - y good thing.
wood-bird, the hymn of the sea; hymn of the sea; hymn of the sea.

No. 39.

I want this song to go faster, so I mark it *Allegro*, (pronounced *Allaygrow,*) the musical word for quick, lively. The way we have been singing would be called *moderato*, (pronounced *modarahtow*.)

ALLEGRO

Sol,   sol,   sol,   la,   sol,   sol,   sol,   la,   sol,   sol,   sol.

1. Haste ye a - way! haste ye a - way! For it is
2. Haste to the wild, maid - en and child; Where is the

La,   la,   la,   si,   si,   si,   do,   si,   la,   sol,   sol,   sol,   la.

com - ing, 'tis com - ing,   'tis com-ing, O haste ye a - way,
drum-ming, the chirp and the hum-ming; O there Spring hath smil'd.

Sol,   sol,   sol,   la,   sol,   sol   sol,   la,   la,   la,   si,   si,   si,   do.

Haste ye a - way, For it is com-ing, the beau-ti-ful day.
Haste to the wild, Spring time is com-ing, sweet maid-en and child.

No. 40.

I want the next song to go slow, so I mark it *Andante*, which in music means rather slow.

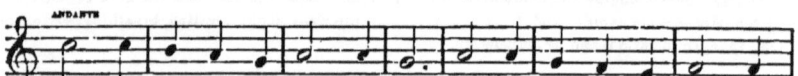

ANDANTE

Do,   do,   si,   la,   sol,   la,   la,   sol,   la,   la,   sol,   fa,   mi,   fa,   fa.

1. Slow - ly sound-ing a - long the dell, Hear the tones of the eve - ning
2. Soft - ly tril - leth a child-ish lay, Birds and bees 'mid the blos -soms

Mi,   re,   mi,   fa,   mi,   re,   mi,   fa,   sol,   fa,   mi,   mi,   re,   re,   do.

bell, Rest from la - bor its num-bers tell; Its plain-tive num-bers tell.
gay, These we heard when the morn was grey; A sim - ple, bird- like lay.

What does allegro mean? Moderato? Andante? To which department do these terms belong? That is, have they to do with the length of sounds, or the pitch of sounds, or the power of sounds?

Make four measures of time again, but now let them be long enough to put four counts into each measure, instead of three; that is say one, two, three, four, in each.

CHAPTER IX.

Now while I count, you may sing quarter notes to the syllable *la*, on the pitch *G*, four in each measure.

This is QUADRUPLE MEASURE.

No. 41.

La, la, la, la, la, la, la, la, la, la, la, la, la, la, la, la.

Ev-'ry step that we are tak-ing,Shows some prog-ress we are mak-ing.
Ev-'ry rill that seeks the riv-er, Swells the cur-rent on and ev-er.

Now sing a half and two quarter notes in each measure; pitch *G*; syllable *la*. I'll count.

No. 42.

La, la, la, la, la, la, la, la, la, la, la, la.

Half, quar-ter, half, quar-ter, half, quar-ter, half, quar-ter.
O, Wil-lie, no oth-er, sings like you, dear broth-er.

Now a dotted half and quarter in each measure.

No. 43

La, la, la, la, la, la, la, la.

Help me, help me sing this long note.
Fare-well, Fare-well sum-mer ro-ses,
On your sweet dust snow re-po-ses.

Now fill each measure with a single sound; same pitch; same syllable. This length is called a WHOLE NOTE, and is represented thus: **No. 44.**

Whole note; long sound.

Shall we put the whole note among the things of Rhythmics, Melodics, or Dynamics? Where shall we put the new measure? How many lengths have we now? Name them.

No. 45.

If we wish to have a piece of music go a little faster tnan moderato, yet not quite so fast as Allegro, we mark it *Allegretto*.

Do, do, do, do, re, re, re, re, mi, mi, mi, mi, fa,

1 E - ven meas-ure, what a pleas - ure, 'Tis the time to keep;
2. Roll for - ev - er, rap - id riv - er, Thine a sweet - er song.

Sol, sol, sol, sol, la, la, la, la, si, si, si, si, do.

High - er mount - ing to the count-ing, As we on - ward sweep;
On thy bo - som hill - side blos - som Sea - ward floats a - long.

No. 46.

Sol, sol, sol, la, la, la, sol, fa, mi, re, do, do.

1. Bir - die sweet, Bir - die sweet, Where may you be go - ing?
2. Bir - die sweet, Bir - die sweet, When you are re - turn - ing.

Re, re, re, mi, mi, mi, fa, sol, la, si, do, do.

From the North, Has - ten South, Fear - ful winds are blow - ing;
Come to me, Let me see What new songs you're learn - ing.

No. 47.

Do, do, do, do, si, si, do, do, do, do, si, si,

1. I toss you my ball, Then you toss back to me. Now
2. Throw back to me now, Shall I show you just how A

Do, do, do, do, si, la, sol, la, sol, fa, mi, re, do.

to and fro, O what a throw!'Tis lodg'd up in a tree.
boy should play? This is the way; The way for boys to play.

No. 48.

Let one voice or a few voices sing the words of this exercise, *Mezzo*, and the remainder of the class the syllables of the scale as they occur, *forte*, all joining where it is marked *Chorus*

The first step of the stair-way Was made of un-bak'd bread. The

second was a sun-beam That shone from o-ver-head. The

third, I stepp'd up-on my-self! The fourth was dis-tant, far. The

fifth, just like a spir-it seem'd; Sixth, half the Turk's Al-lah! The

seventh was like the o-cean wave, The rock-ing, toss-ing main. So

to the eighth a leap I gave; 'Twas un-bak'd bread a-gain. I

hur-ried down an-oth-er flight, Just like the one be-fore! Yet

folks of note, both black and white, Climb these strange stair-ways o'er.

CHAPTER X.

No. 49.

Make two measures of time, but with six counts in each. Now I will count for you to sing quarter notes; pitch *G;* syllable *la.* This is called SEXTUPLE MEASURE.

| La, | la, | la, | la, | la, | la, | la, | la, | la, | la, | la, | la. |

Long-est   of   meas - ures   this   one   of   the   six   parts   is.

Sing sextuple measures while I count, and make three quarters and a dotted half, in each.

No. 50.

| La, | la, la, la, | la, la, la, la, | la, la, la, la, | la, la, la, la. |

Oh! come and play, Sweet lit-tle flow'rs, An-na and May; Play-mates of ours.

Now sing four measures again, and fill each measure with ⌀ • | ⌀ • | ⌀ • | ⌀ • |
a single sound. This length is called a DOTTED WHOLE NOTE.   La,   la,   la,   la.

No. 51.

ALLEGRO

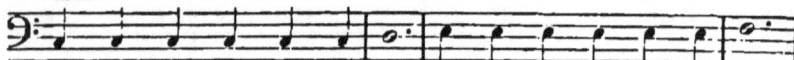

·Do,   do,   do,   do,   do,   do,   re,   mi,   mi,   mi,   mi,   mi,   mi.   fa,
Clear   and firm,   hold   the tones long; Take the breath well to   sus - tain;
1. Where the sweet - est   dai - sies bloom; Where the dews of   eve - ning   fall,
2. Heard we   not   at   clos - ing   day,   An - gel whis-pers soft - ly   call?

Sol,   sol,   sol,   sol   sol,   sol,   la,   si,   si,   si,   si,   si,   si,   do.
Strive   in   each line   of   the song, Time, and good tune   to   main-tain.
Is   a   lit - tle gras - sy tomb, Is   the grave of   lit - tle Paul;
When we   laid our hopes   a - way, In   the grave of   lit - tle Paul.

No. 52.

ALLEGRO

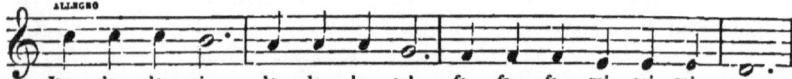

Do,   do,   do,   si,   la,   la,   la,   sol,   fa,   fa,   fa,   mi,   mi,   mi,   re.
1. Where are they gone, Wil-liam and John? Why have they left us   to - day?
2. Beau - ti - ful streams! How like our dreams, On thro' the val-ley they wind;

Mi, mi, mi, fa, sol, sol, sol, la, sol, la, sol, fa, mi, re, do.

O - ver the hills, Down by the rills, They and their boats pass a - way.
There at their plays, See our es-trays, We are the girls "left be-hind."

To which department do Sextuple measure and the dotted whole note belong? How many quarter notes are equal to one-half? How many to a whole? To a dotted whole? How many kinds of measure or time, have we? (&c., &c., reviewing what has been practiced.)

CHAPTER XI.

Count four measures in double time. Now again, but while you are counting, make motions of the hand like this, (the teacher counts and beats, down, up, while speaking.) This is called BEATING TIME. Do not move the whole arm—only hands—and make the motions prompt, letting the hand stop at each point until the time of the count has passed, thus: (Teacher gives example.) Do not let the hand hit anything to make a noise. When I say ready, all raise hands; and when I say commence, all begin to count and beat, *moderato.*

Now try beating and singing at the same time; four measures; quarter notes; pitch *G*; syllable *la.* Ready; commence. (This is repeated until it is well done, if there is anything wrong.) Now beat again and sing half notes. Ready; commence. Now again, and sing first a measure of quarter notes, then a half, and so on.

Turn back to No. 27 and see if you can sing this and beat the time. After singing to No. 34, the teacher says: Count four measures in triple time, and beat thus: (teacher counts and beats down, left, up.) Now sing quarter notes, and beat. Try dotted half notes, Now a half and quarter in each measure. This is hard, and you will probably have to practice it sometime before you can do it well. Make the motions promptly and gracefully.

After singing from No. 38 to No. 40, and beating the time, the teacher introduces beating quadruple measure (down, left, right, up,) in a similar way, and the pupils beat and sing from No. 45 to No. 48, and then the beating for sextuple measure is introduced with the motions as follows: 1st. The hand half down. 2nd. The rest of the way. 3rd. Left. 4th. Right. 5th. Half way up. 6th. The remainder, or down, down, left, right, up, up.

This is the most difficult measure to beat, and it will be well to practice longer with the counting, and the singing of quarter notes, than in the others. When the class is ready, let them try from No. 51 to No. 52, singing and beating.

To which department in music does beating time belong? Beating time is very useful to help form correct habits of keeping time, but may be dispensed with, after a certain amount of progress has been made.

CHAPTER XII.

All sing the sound we have learned to the syllable *do, re, mi, &c.,* as I call their scale names. (We print the figures instead of the words one, two, three, &c., to save room.) 1, 2, 3, 4, 5, 6, 7, 8, and 7, 6, 5, 4, 3, 2, 1, 2, 1, 2, 3, 2, 3, 2, 3, 4, 3, 4, 5, 4, 5, 4, 5, 6, 5, 6, 7, 6, 7, 6, 7, 8, 7, 8, 7, 6, 7, 6, 7, 6, 5, 6, 5, 4, 5, 4, 5, 4, 3, 4, 3, 2, 3, 2, 3, 2, 1, 2, 3, 4, 5, 6, 7————————8. (The teacher waits a little after they have sung 7, to see if any sing 8 without direction. This sometimes causes a little amusement.) 8, 7, 6, 5, 4, 3, 2————————1.

All sing 1 again—think of 2. (Don't think aloud.) Sing 3, 1, 3, 1, 3, 3, 3, 1————1, 3—think of 4—sing 5—think of 4. Sing 3, 1. 3, 5, 5, 5, 5, 1, 3, 5, 3, 5, 3, 5, 3, 1————1, 3, 5—think of 6—think of 7. Sing 8, 8, 8—think of 7—think of 6. Sing 5, 8, 5, 8, 5, 8, 1, 3, 5, 8, 8 5, 3, 1. The teacher continues this exercise as the pupils require. What we have been doing is called SKIPPING. *Does it belong to Rhythmics, Melodics, or Dynamics?*

No. 53.—ROUND.

Do, mi, sol, do, sol, do.
Now come on, you can - not catch us, For we have the start, you know;

Do, sol, mi, do.
Hear them say what we are say - ing, As we on to - geth - er go.

When the preceding lesson has been sung by all together, the teacher says: We may make of this what is called a ROUND, by singing it over and over, without stopping the beats, or losing the time between the ending or beginning. You may try it, and while you are singing I will say *piano, mezzo,* or *forte,* as I want the dynamics of the lesson to be varied. When I raise my hand, it will be your signal to stop when you have sung to the end of the piece. Ready; commence. (The class sing it three or four times, the teacher giving the dynamic directions as he thinks best.)

Now do the same again, only do not all begin together. (The teacher divides the class into two equal parts in any convenient way.) Let this half of the class commence first, and the other half commence when the first have sung one measure. After you have commenced, keep right on until I give the signal, and then stop when you get to the end of the piece.

The teacher may now divide his class into three sections, and sing this piece, each section coming in one measure after the other, and when the signal is given, ending one after the other. In fact, it may be sung by four, five, six, seven, or eight sections, in the same way, or by each pupil in the class coming in one measure after the preceding.

No. 54.

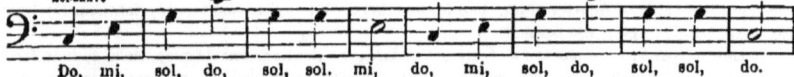

Do, mi, sol, do, sol, sol. mi, do, mi, sol, do, sol, sol, do.
1. Sons of Free-dom wake the song, Be the ech -oes loud and long.
2. Lo! the curse hath pass'd a - way! Praise the Lord for this, for aye.

Sol, sol, mi, mi, do, do, sol, do, mi, sol, do, sol, sol, do.
Tell-ing of the great *To Be,* Breath-ing notes of proph - e - cy.
Hon-ors now and ev - er bring, To our Sav - ior and our King.

No. 55.

Do, mi, sol, do, mi, sol, do, sol, do, mi, sol, do, sol, mi, do.

Mer - ri - ly, Mer - ri - ly bound - ing Off to the wood-land a - way,

Do, mi, sol, do, mi, sol, do, sol, do, mi, sol, do, sol, mi, do.

For the bold horn is re-sound - ing, And the great stag is at bay.

All sing four measures in double time, pitch G, a half note in each measure, *moderato*, using the word *Hark!*

No. 56.

Hark! hark! hark! hark!

If you wished to listen to anything, would you say *hark* in this way, or would you speak it shorter? Will all give four measures again, and in each measure sing *hark*, but let the sound continue only half through the measure or during one beat. Be silent in the last part of the measure, only occupy it by the beat. This is called *resting*, and the sign for silence during one beat is called a QUARTER REST.

No. 57.

Hark! hark! hark! hark!

What kind of note is a quarter rest equal to in length?

Sing four measures again with a quarter rest and a quarter note in each, but let the rest come first:

No. 58.

Hark! hark! hark! hark!

Now four triple measures, one sound in each, same pitch, same word. *How many parts has each triple measure?* Let the sound occupy the first part of each measure, and the rest the other two. This kind of a rest is called a HALF REST. It is represented by a little oblong form, as you see, *just above* a line.

No. 59.

Hark! hark! hark! hark!

How many beats, or parts of a measure does the half rest occupy? What kind of a note is it equal to?

Try these four measures again, but let the rest come first:

No. 60.

Hark! hark! hark! hark!

Now again, and let each measure have first a quarter rest, then a quarter note, then a quarter rest. You may have to practice some time before you can beat and sing this right.

No. 61.

Hark!   hark!   hark!   hark!

Now give me four quadruple measures, with a quarter note in the first part of each, and a rest filling the remainder. This kind of rest is called a DOTTED HALF REST.

No. 62.

Hark!   hark!   hark!   hark!

Now again, but let the rest come first.

No. 63.

Hark!   hark!   hark!   hark!

Now let each measure contain, as follows; quarter rest, quarter note, half rest :

No. 64.

Hark!   hark!   hark!   hark!

Now, as follows; half rest, quarter note, quarter rest :

No. 65.

Hark!   hark!   hark!   hark!

Now let the first measure be filled with four quarter notes, and the second with a rest. Let the third measure be like the first, and the fourth like the second. Syllable *la*. This rest is represented by a character like the half rest, only just below the line instead of just above it. It is called a WHOLE REST.

No. 66.

Now be si - lent,   Yes, be si - lent.

Now four measures of sextuple time. Fill the first with quarter notes, the second with a rest, the third with quarter notes, and the fourth with a rest. This is called a DOTTED WHOLE REST.

No. 67.

What is that com-ing ? hark!   O, it is ver - y dark.

It might be mentioned here, that when a measure rest occurs in any kind of time, a whole rest is used to represent it. But anything that is told to learners will not be likely to be remembered unless it is put into something for them to do, as it is only by *doing* that we really acquire. *Do rests belong to rhythmics, melodics or dynamics ?*

No. 68.

Sol, sol, sol, sol, la, la, la, la, . la, sol, do, do.
Look! look! look! the sol - dier boys are march-ing; Left, left,

do, do, sol, sol, do, do, re, mi, fa, sol, la, si, do,
left, left, left, left, left, So on - ward al - to - geth - er move,

Do, re, mi, fa, sol, la si, do, do, sol, do.
Un - til they hear the word they love. Halt! halt! halt!

Round, in three parts. Let each division sing two measures before the next commences. Sing it over until it goes well, all together, then divide into three sections.

No. 69.—Round.

1 2 3

Do, sol, do, sol, do, do, mi, mi, mi, mi, mi, mi.
John - ny! John - ny! What? what? So we keep call - ing him.

No. 70.

Sol, mi, sol, mi, do, re, mi, fa, sol, la, sol,
1. Sing now, rest now, Sing - ing is a pleas - ant task;
2. Work now, play now, Thus our task should all be done;
3. Sleep now, wake now, This the way our life must go;

sol, la, si, do, sol, la, si, do, si, la, sol, fa, mi, re, do.
Let us try to do our best now, That is all our teach-ers ask.
Not too long at la - bor stay now; Life must have its share of fun.
Night must fall, and morn-ing break now; Don't you see it must be so.

CHAPTER XIV.

Listen, and tell, if you can, whether I sing double, triple, quadruple or sextuple measure. The teacher sings perhaps twelve quarter notes, pitch G, syllable *la*, without beating or accenting, or in any way indicating the measure. The class will not be able to tell with certainty. The teacher sings again, still without beating, but now accenting the first note of each measure. After the class see that this is double measure, and have done the same thing themselves, the teacher says: It seems to be natural to make the first sound of each measure a little louder than the others, and this is called ACCENT. The notes which are sung louder are called ÁCCENTED NOTES, and those that are sung after, UNACCENTED NOTES. Turn back, and sing No. 27, and sing it, noticing this fact.

The teacher now sings some triple measures, manifesting them by accent, without beating. After the class have done the same, they sing No. 38. The teacher then shows that in quadruple time the accent occurs not only in the first part, as in double and triple, but slightly on the third.

All sing No. 45. The teacher then shows that sextuple measure is naturally accented on the first and fourth parts—more on the first, and less on the fourth—and all sing No. 51.

You know that when we speak or read we make some words or syllables louder than others, especially in poetry. All say together, "How sweet and calm the evening air," and notice this. Now let us set these words to music. The music says we must accent the first note in each measure. Let us see how that will agree with the emphasis of the words:

No. 71.

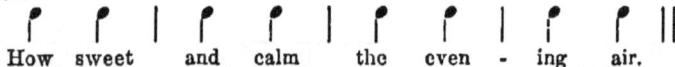

How sweet   and calm   the   even - ing   air.

You see there is a conflict. *In speaking the first two words, which is naturally louder, " How" or " sweet !"* Then we must contrive to have "sweet" come to the accented note of the measure. We may do it in this way:

No. 72.

How sweet and   calm the   even - ing   air.

But it is common to begin a piece of music with a part of a measure, in order to accommodate the emphasis of the words and make it agree with the musical accent. When this is done, it is always noticed, that the last measure of the piece will not be full also, and that the last and first together will make as much as one full measure.

In singing this and other lessons of this kind, commence at the right place in the second measure, that is, beat and describe a full measure beside the one in which the song commences.

No. 73.

How   sweet   and   calm   the   even - ing   air.

What kind of measure has an accent that would agree with the emphasis of the following words?
"Gladly we welcome the summer again." Sing it to the pitch G. *How do you think the movement ought to be; andante, moderato, allegretto or allegro?*

No. 74.

Glad - ly　　we　　wel - come　　the　　sum - mer　　a - gain.

Supposing the words were "Yes, gladly," &c., would you commence on the full measure, or on the second or third part? Sing it. If the words were, "O, yes, gladly," &c., on which part would you commence? Sing it. *To which department does commencing on different parts of the measure belong? In which department will you put accent?*

The large bars of the following piece of music do not indicate measures, but divide the piece into sections. *How many sections is this song divided into?*

No. 75.

ALLEGRETTO

Sol,　do,　do,　do,　sol,　la,　si,　do,　do,　mi,　mi,　mi,　re,　do,

1. The swal-low flies a - bove the trees, Then skims a - long the ground ;
2. So up-ward may our song take flight, So down-ward safe-ly　go;

Sol,　do,　do,　do,　sol,　la,　si,　do,　do,　mi,　mi,　mi,　re,　do.

First up-ward borne up - on the breeze, Then down where flow'rs a-bound:
Not bawl-ing out with all our might, But sing-ing sweet and low:

Sol,　la,　la,　la,　sol,　la,　si,　do,　do,　si,　si,　si,　la,　sol,

He dips and flut-ters, stops and flies, Where sil-ver stream-lets flow;
And when the waves of mel - o - dy Go sway-ing here and there,

Sol,　do,　do,　do,　sol,　la,　si,　do,　do,　mi,　mi,　mi,　re,　do.

Then up-ward soars to-ward the skies, While we stand here be - low.
We fol - low when they lead us high, And then de-scend with care.

How many of the sections in the previous are just alike as to the music? Sometimes when sections are alike, we can save room by making them so as to have the music repeated. The dots just before the double bar do this. D. C. stand for the words *Da Capo*, which mean sing the first section again. FINE means *the end.*

No. 76.

ALLEGRETTO   FINE.

The swal-low flics a - bove the trees, Then skims a - long the ground; }
First up-ward borne up-on the breeze, Then down where flow'rs a-bound: }
D. C. Then up-ward soars to-ward the skies, While we stand here be - low.

D. C.

He dips and flut-ters, stops and flies, Where sil-ver stream-lets flow;

CHAPTER XV.

Sing the scale—half notes, syllables *do, re, mi*, &c. *How many key-notes are there in this scale?*

Now let us make another scale, by commencing at the upper key-note, and singing upward. This, you see, will be making our upper key-note the lower key-note of a new scale. Sing half notes to the syllable *la*, Do not strain your voices, as it is not necessary to sing the whole of this scale.

After the class have sung what they can of this scale, or the teacher has perhaps manifested it on some instrument, he says this scale is so similar to the other that its pitches have the same names, and it is sung with the same syllables. The pitch of the lower key-note, or one, is named C; the next pitch, D; the next, E, and so on. Sing in this new scale as I call, using syllables *do, re, mi*, &c., 1, 1, 2, 2, 3, 3, 2, 2, 1, 2, 3, 4, 5, 4, 3, 2, 1. (If the teacher thinks best, the higher tones of this scale may be sung, but straining young voices should very seldom be done.)

What degree of the treble staff represents the pitch of the lower key-note of our new scale? Which line or space stands for D? Which for E? F? G?

Now we are at the highest degree of this staff, but we may add more degrees if we want them. The degree which stands for A is named the FIRST ADDED LINE ABOVE. That which stands for B is named the FIRST ADDED SPACE ABOVE. (There is but *one* space above and but *one* space below, just as there is but one first space, one second space, &c., and there are no added spaces until there are added lines.) That which stands for C, the upper key-note, is the SECOND ADDED LINE ABOVE.

No. 77.

C,	D,	E,	F,	G,	A,	B,	C.
1,	2,	3,	4,	5,	6,	7,	8.
Do,	re,	mi,	fa,	sol,	la,	si,	do.

How many pitches does our new scale contain ? How many are new to us ? To which department does this scale belong ?

It may here be well, if there is an instrument at hand, to play still another scale above, and explain, that the upper key-note of this new scale may be taken as the lower key-note of a still higher scale, and that the pitches are named as before. It may also be explained, that the pitches are represented by more added degrees of the staff, and that these pitches, being above the voice, are only used in instrumental music.

We will call the first scale that we learned the MIDDLE SCALE, and the new one the UPPER SCALE.

No. 78.

Do, do, re, re, mi, mi, re, re, mi, fa, sol, fa, mi, re, do.

1. Sing a lay, Bright Queen of May; June waits the crown You will lay down.
2. But your reign, Will come a - gain; So do not mourn, Your pow-er gone.

No. 79.

Do, do, do, re, re, re, mi, mi, mi, fa,

1. Out of the hea - vy clouds, Som - ber and brown,
2. Lov - ing - ly, spark - ling - ly, Laugh - ing - ly falls,

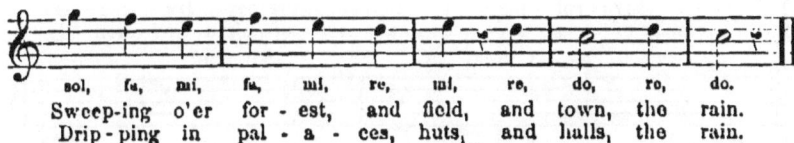

sol, fa, mi, fa, mi, re, mi, re, do, re, do.

Sweep-ing o'er for - est, and field, and town, the rain.
Drip - ping in pal - a - ces, huts, and halls, the rain.

All sing our old acquaintance, the middle scale, again, but commence at eight and sing down in half notes, syllables do, si, la, &c. Now let the lower key-note, or one that you have just sung, be regarded as the upper key-note, or eight, of a LOWER SCALE, and sing down. It is not likely that any of you can sing to the lower key-note of this scale; but some instruments can go down, and some of its pitches we can use.

The pitches of this scale are named just like the others—eight is named C; seven, B; six, A; and so on, and the syllables apply in the same manner. All sing syllables as I call for the sounds of this lower scale—8, 8, 7, 7, 6, 6, 5, 5, 5, 5, 6, 7, 8.

If eight, or C, is represented by the first added line below, what will stand for seven, or B ? What for six, or A ? &c. But if you take the base staff, where the second space stands for C, what will stand for B ? What for A ? G ? F ? E ? D ? C ? (The teacher may show, if convenient, that an instrument can make a still lower scale.)

3

No. 80.

C,	B,	A,	G,	F,	E,	D,	C.
8,	7,	6,	5,	4,	3,	2,	1.
Do,	si,	la,	sol,	fa,	mi,	re,	do.

It would be well here to have the class become familiar with as much of the upper and lower scales as their voices can reach, as well as the lines and spaces of the staff that represent them. This can be done by pointing to the degrees of the staff that represent the new pitches, the class singing syllables, or such words as the teacher may select.

No. 81.

Do, do, si, si, la, la, sol, la, la, si, si, do, re, do.

1. Deep-er, deep-er, deep-er down In the low-er scale we go.
2. Do not stoop, nor nod, nor frown, While the stead-y meas-ures flow.

No. 82.

Do, do, do, si, si, si, la, la, la, sol, la, si, do,

1. Heav-i-ly roll-ing all o-ver the earth, Hush-ing the
2. Dark clouds of va-por and shad-ows of night, Sud-den-ly

1ST TIME.   2D TIME.

si, do, re, do, re, mi, re, do, mi, re, do.

sounds of re-joic-ing and mirth;
fell on the (*omit*).................ar-rows of light.

In the following lessons name first, the pitches, mentioning also which scale each pitch is in—middle, upper or lower. Give also the scale names.

No. 83.

Do, re, do, do, re, do, do, re, mi, do, re, mi,

1. One, two, one, one, two, one; O what fun, O what fun:
2. Try a-gain, try a-gain; 'Till 'tis plain, 'till 'tis plain;

Do, re, mi, fa, mi, re, do, do, re, mi, fa, mi, re, do.
Now we have a larg - er scale, Let us not in sing - ing, fail.
Run-ning up and run - ning down, Smile each one, but nev - er frown.

No. 84.

Do, re, mi, fa, sol, do, re, mi, fa, sol,
1. Now we have to try Go - ing ver - y high;
2. Once more we will see If we reach the G;

do, si, la, sol, do, do, si, la, sol. do.
Now then down a - gain Goes the mer - ry strain;
Now re - turn a - gain To the low - er strain.

No. 85.

Do, do, si, la, sol, la, si, do, si, la, sol, sol, la, la,
1. The time now is trip - le, and we must look out, Tho' low, wo
2. That was pret - ty good, but may be bet - ter yet; Once more now

si, si, do, mi, sol, do, do, si, la, sol, la, si, do.
go up, up, up, up, Take care now what you are a - bout.
o'er this piece we go, Please greet us, when per - fect we get.

No. 86.

Do, do, re, re, mi, mi, re, do, si, la, si, do,
1. Why dear com-rades, on - ly see How low down we are;
2. 'Tis so odd, we'd bet - ter try How 'twill go once more;

do,   do,   re,   re,   mi,   mi,   re,   do,   si,   la,   si,   do.

What a   fun - ny   mel - o - dy,   Down and up   so   far.

Don't you like   it,   low and high,   Bet - ter than be - fore ?

No. 87.

Do,   re,   mi,   fa,   sol,   la,   si,   do,   re,   mi,   do,   re,   si,   do,

1. We give our whole at - ten - tion now to sing - ing what we see;

2. Try once a - gain, re - mem - ber not to strain the voice at all;

mi,   fa,   mi,   re,   do,   si,   la,   sol,   fa,   mi,   do,   re,   si,   do.

When we are per - fect, oh, how glad our teach - ers kind will be.

We've ris - en now, and pleas - ant - ly we let our voi - ces fall.

No. 88.

Do,   re,   sol,   sol,   re,   sol,   sol,   mi,   sol,   sol,   do,   do,   re,   sol,   sol,

1. Once more tri - ple time, 'tis our pleas-ure to greet,'Tis down ver - y

2. O, playmates,dear playmates, when les-sons are done,'Twill then be a

re,   sol,   sol,   mi,   sol,   sol,   do,   sol,   la,   si,   do,   sol,   la,   si,   do.

low, but it still may be sweet; Here comes a rest, Let's do our best.

good time for play and for fun; Let us at - tend Now to the end.

No. 89.

Do,   mi,   do,   sol,   do,   sol,   do,   sol,   do,   do,   sol,   mi,   do.

Do not hur - ry,   Do not wor - ry,   We shall win at last.

CHAPTER XVI.

The teacher starts at the pitch G, and sings down as far as five *in the key of G*—half notes to the syllable *la*. Of course, he sings F sharp instead of F, but it sounds so natural that the class probably do not notice that a new tone has been introduced; and, as they readily sing the same tones when called upon, are perhaps surprised to learn that the pitch F has been thrown aside, and a new pitch substituted.

After practicing upon these four tones, by imitating the examples of the teacher, who gives them out in a variety of ways (without skipping), the class are informed that the new pitch is higher than F and lower than G, and is named F sharp, and not the F that they have been singing. The teacher then says, sing half notes, syllable *la*, to the pitches that I name. G, F sharp, G, F sharp, E, D, E, F sharp, G, A, B, A, G.

Now listen while I sing, and end on our old key-note C. The teacher then sings G, A, B, A, G, F sharp, G, F sharp, E, D, C, and says, *Is this a good stopping place or home?* The class will readily perceive that C is not now a satisfactory key-note, and the teacher says, this throwing away F, and taking another pitch in its place, makes a great change in our music; and as C is no longer a good key-note, let us try to find one that is. When I come to it, you may raise your hands. He then sings as follows (dwelling on the tones toward the last): G, A, B, A, G, F sharp, E, D, C, D, C, E, F sharp, G. At G, all will probably raise hands, and the teacher says, Yes; when F sharp is brought in among the tones instead of F, the key-note is G.

Now let us make a scale calling this key-note one, singing *do* to one, *re* to two, *mi* to three, and so on. This scale goes quite high, perhaps higher than some of you can sing easily.

Let us take one again, and considering it the upper key-note of a lower scale, sing down.

After exercising sufficiently on these two scales, by calling for their tones by pitch names and scale names (G, A, B, A, or one, two, three, two, &c.) the teacher explains that the term KEY is sometimes given to the tones] of a scale. The key of C, for example, consists of the tones A, B, C, D, E, F and G, with this difference, that these tones in any order, either of succession or combination, are still the key of C, while only a certain order of succession puts them into the form of the *scale* of C.

The key of G consists of the tones A, B, C, D, E, F sharp and G, in any order or combination they may have, while they form the *scale* of G, only when they follow each other in intervals of seconds. We therefore, speak of a tune or piece of music as being in the *key* of G, or the *key* of C, rather than in the *scale* of G or C—the key-note, of course, giving the name of the key.

He then points to the treble staff, and says, the line and space which stand for the pitch named F, are of no use to us as they are now, for this key, because we have no such pitch to represent. They can, however, easily be made to stand for the new pitch through their entire length by placing a character called a SHARP upon them at the beginning, thus:

No. 90.

The pitch F is now not here represented, but instead of it this new pitch that is half way between F and G. But this new pitch is a very pleasant and easy one to sing, as we have ascertained.

Sing half notes to syllables, *do, re, mi,* &c., as I point. After exercising sufficiently on the staff, the teacher says, it is customary to put a sharp on but one of the degrees that stand for F in each staff, the other change is understood; for example, a sharp on the fifth line indicates that the first space is to stand for F sharp also, although a different one.

The sharp so placed is called the SIGNATURE or sign of the key. It happens in this key that the tones most convenient to sing comprise a part of the upper and a part of the lower scales, as follows. This going to a new key is called TRANSPOSITION.

No. 91.

```
        G, F sharp, E,  D,  E, F sharp, G,  A,  B,  C,  D,  E,  D,  G.
        8,    7,    6,  5,  6,   7,     1,  2,  3,  4,  5,  6,  5,  1.
        Do,  si,   la, sol, la, si,    do, re, mi, fa, sol, la, sol, do.
```

I would call the attention of teachers and musical people to the fact, that it is much easier to sing F sharp as one of the tones of a diatonic scale than as a chromatic tone; and much easier to represent it by modifying the line or space of the staff once for all throughout the entire tune, than to do so only for a measure or part of a measure, as is done by an accidental—consequently, that the key of G properly comes before the introduction of sharp four, or any other tone of the chromatic scale.

What is the name of this new family of tones? (*Ans.* The key of G.) Give me the names of the members of this family, or in other words the pitches of which it is composed. *What is the signature of the key of G?*

No. 92.

```
        Do,    re,   mi,   fa,   sol,     do,   re,   mi,   fa,   sol,
```

```
        do,   si,   la,   sol,   do,   si,   la,   sol,   do,   re,   mi,   re,   do.
```

No. 93.

```
        Do,    si,   si,   si,   do,   do,   do,   si,   la,   sol,   do,   mi,
        1. Come,  Rov - er,  old   Rov - er,   and   fol - low   our   slid - ing;
        2. But   sparo  us    a    so - lo    of   bow-wows—it   may   be
```

do, si, si, si, do, do, do, si, la, sol, do, do.

Your skates are the good ones, of na - ture's pro - vid - ing.
Your mu - sic, old fel - low, will wake up the ba - by.

No. 94.

Do, re, mi; fa, do, re, mi, fa, mi, re, fa, mi, re, do,

1. One, two, three, four, one, two, three, Sing the notes a - long with me;
2. One, two, three, four, one, two, three, Let your voice be full and free;
3. One, two, three, four, one, two, three, Oh! what sound can sweet - er be!

do, re, mi, fa, do, re, mi, fa, mi, re, sol, mi, re, do.

One, two, three, four, keep the time, Let our tune-ful voi - ces chime.
One, two, three, four, let it sing, Sing now, hap-py chil - dren, sing.
One, two, three, four, if you try, You will learn this mel - o - dy.

No. 95.

Mi, mi, mi, re, do, sol, do, re, mi, mi, mi, re, do, mi, sol,

1. Heed the sounds that we are giv-ing, While we skip thus: one, three, five;
2. See the joy - ous squir-rel spring-ing, Watch his skips now, one, three, five;
3. Well this les - son you are learn - ing, Well you sing your one, three, five;

mi, mi, mi, re, do, sol, do, mi, sol, sol, sol, fa, mi, re, do.

List - en, chil-dren, list - en, striv-ing Well to learn the sounds we give.
On the loft - y branch now swing-ing, Soon he high - er up will live.
Soon to oth-er mu - sic turn-ing You the oth - er sounds shall give.

No. 96.

8, 5, 1, 3, 8, 5, 1, 3, 5, 8, 8, 5, 3, 8, 5, 3, 1.
Do, sol, do, mi, do, sol, do, mi, sol, do, do, sol, mi, do, sol, mi, do.

No. 97.

Sol,   do,   do,   re,   re,   mi,   mi,   re,   mi,   sol,   do,   mi,   re,   do,

1. Two   rob - in red-breasts built their nest Up   in   a   ma - ple   tree;
The   one was brood-ing o'er her young, The oth - er sang with   glee:
2. Once   on   a   sum - mer morn the sun   Was shin - ing   in   the   sky;
The   rob - in said, "My   lit - tle dears, 'Tis time you learn to   fly:
3. I   know a girl,   and who she is   I'll tell you by and   by;
When moth-er says,   "Do this, or that," She says, "What for," and "Why?"

mi,   sol,   mi,   fa,   re,   mi,   do,   re,   sol,   do,   sol,   do,   sol,   do.

And   all   the   lit - tle young ones said, "Wee, wee, wee, wee, wee, wee."
And   all   the   lit - tle young ones said, "I'll try, I'll try, I'll try."
She'd   be   a   bet - ter girl by far,   If she would say, "I'll try."

CHAPTER XVII.

All sing G, half note, syllable *la*. Now F sharp. E. D. Now tell me the names of the pitches as I sing them. The teacher sings D, E, F sharp, G, A and B. The class give the names readily so far. The teacher then says, I will now throw aside C, and take C sharp, a pitch which is half way between C and D, notice how pleasantly and easily it comes in.

After giving it, the teacher commences again at D, and sings, the class naming the pitches. D, E, F sharp, G, A, B, C sharp, D. All sing the same.

Introducing C sharp instead of C, makes another key. Let us find the key-note.

After this is done, the teacher says, name the members of this new family, of which D is the father or key-note. Now sing as I call, quarter notes, syllable *la*. D, E, F sharp, E, F sharp, G, A, B, C sharp, D, C sharp, B, A, D.

Now, as I give the scale names, sing quarter notes with syllables, *do, re, mi*, &c. 1, 2, 3, 4, 5, 6, 7, 8, 7, 6, 5, 5, 3, 3, 1.

The staff is made to stand for the key of D by *two sharps*, placed as follows:

No. 98.

D,   E,   F sharp,   G,   A,   B,   C sharp,   D.
1,   2,   3,   4,   5,   6,   7,   8.
Do,   re,   mi,   fa,   sol,   la,   si,   do.

After exercising in this key, by pointing as in the previous keys, the teacher says: *What is a key in music?* (*Ans.* A family of tones.) *How many of these families or keys have been introduced to us thus far?* (*Ans.* Three.) *What was the first one?* (*Ans.* The key of C.) *The next? This one? What is the signature of the key of C?* (*Ans.* Natural.) *What is the signature of the key of G? What of the key of D?*

Before singing the following lessons, name the clef, signature, key, kind of time, and give the pitch and scale names and syllables of each.

No. 99.

Do, do, do, do, do, re, re, mi, mi, mi, mi, mi, fa,

1. Com - ing thro' clouds and dark-ness, Com - ing thro' sleet and rain,
2. Tho't of the win-t'ry hour— Cheer of the dark-est day—
3. Com - ing a morn of glo - ry, Com - ing a day of rest,
4. Star of the dark - est hour, Beam-ing with death-less ray—

sol, sol, sol, sol, sol, la, la, si, si, si, si, si, do.

Beau - ti - ful month of flow - ers, Hast-'ning to us a - gain.
Com - ing, tho' tem-pests low - er, Beau - ti - ful month of May.
Faith sees its gold - en prom - ise Break thro' the cloud-ed west.
Com - ing, tho' tem-pests low - er, Bless - ed e - ter - nal May.

No. 100.

Do, re, mi, fa, sol, la, sol, mi, la, sol, do, do,

1. Spring has come so fresh and fair, All hail! all hail! And
2. Hear the clear and wel - come song, All hail! all hail! From

re, do, si, la, sol, fa, mi, re, do, mi, sol, sol, do.

sweet - est flow - ers scent the air, On ev - 'ry pass - ing gale.
out the mer - ry, war-bling throng Of wood-land and of vale.

No. 101.—Round.

Do, re, mi, re, do, mi, fa, sol, fa, mi, do, do, do, si, do.

Sing this song with me, Sing it full and free, And we'll mer-ry be.

No. 102.

ALLEGRETTO

Do, do, do, si, si, si, la, la, sol, sol, do, sol, do, sol, do,

1. O, who is down in the well so deep! Say who! say who! say who!
2. How came he down in the well so deep! Say how! say how! say how!

sol, do, do, si, si, si, la, la, sol, sol, do, sol, do, sol, do.

'Tis John-ny Lane, and he's fast a-sleep, That's who, that's who, that's who,
He tho't he'd rest on the wood-en sweep, That's how, that's how, that's how.

No. 103.

Do, do, mi, mi, sol, sol, do, do, do, sol, sol, mi, mi, do,

1. One, and three, and five, and eight, This is all we have to date;
2. Up-ward, up-ward, light-ly bound, Now re - turn we to the ground;

do, do, fa, mi, la, sol, do, re, do, la, sol, mi, re, do.

One, and four, and six, and eight, Here's an - oth - er song to mate.
Up-ward once a - gain we go, And a - gain re - turn be - low.

CHAPTER XVIII.

All sing D, E, F sharp, G, A. Now, if G sharp is in its place, we shall have another key. Listen.
Teacher sings A, G sharp, F sharp, E, D, C sharp, B, A, and says, all do the same. This, as you see,
is the key of A.

Sing as I call (quarter notes, syllable *la*) A, B, C sharp, B, A, G sharp, F sharp, E, D, C sharp, B,
B, A. This is here represented. Sing the same with syllables *do, re, mi, &c.*

No. 104.

A, B, C sharp, B, A, G sharp, F sharp, E, D, C sharp, B, B, A.
1, 2, 3, 2, 8, 7, 6, 5, 4, 3, 2, 2, 1.
Do, re, mi, re, do, si, la, sol, fa, mi, re, re, do.

What are the pitch names of the members of this new family?
Before singing the following lessons, name, as before, the clef, signature, key, kind of time, &c.

No. 105.

Do, mi, sol, do, sol, do, do, si, la, sol, fa, mi, re, do.
One,three, five, eight,five,eight,Eight,seven,six,five, four,three,two,one;

do, si, la, sol, fa, mi, re, do, sol, sol, do.
Sing - ing down is al - ways good fun, yes, good fun.

No. 106.

ALLEGRETTO

Do, do, do, do, do, do, re, re, re, mi, re, do.
1. Fleet as the shad - ows glide, O - ver the ice we fly,
   Swift as the swal - lows ride Un - der the star - ry sky.
2. Blu - est of skies a - bove, Smooth-est of ice be - low,
   Bound to the steel we love, Ev - er and on we go.
3. Shout-ing our words of glee, Sing - ing our songs of mirth,
   Hap - pi - er souls than we Nev - er were found on earth.

Mi, mi, re, re, mi, mi, fa, fa, sol, fa, mi, re, mi, do,
Curl - ing,whirl-ing,Glid - ing,slid - ing, O - ver the ice we sail.
Curl - ing,whirl-ing,Glid - ing,slid - ing, O - ver the ice we sail.
Curl - ing,whirl-ing,Glid - ing,slid - ing, O - ver the ice we sail.

No. 107.

Sol, do, do, re, re, mi, do, mi, fa, mi, re, do, re,
Come, ev - 'ry son and daugh-ter, And join the praise we sing,
D. C. But these are not such pleas-ures That we for them should cry;

Sol, do, do, re, re, mi, do, mi, fa, re, do, si, do,
For clear and spark-ling wa - ter Just from the mead - ow spring
And I'm for tak - ing meas - ures To pass them whol - ly by.

Sol, fa, mi, re, do, fa, mi, mi, re, do, si, do, re,
'Tis true it does not bub - ble, Like ci - der or cham-pagne;

sol, fa, mi, re, do, fa, mi, mi, re, do, si, la. sol.
Nor make you see things dou - ble, Nor of your head com-plain.

CHAPTER XIX.

All sing A. Now G sharp, F sharp, E. We will now make a new key, by taking away D, and putting D sharp in its place. See if you can tell what pitches I sing—I will commence with E. The teacher then sings the scale of E, the pupils naming the pitches:

No. 108.

E, F sharp, G sharp, A, B, C sharp, D sharp, E.
1, 2, 3, 4, 5, 6, 7, 8.
Do, re, mi, fa, sol, la, si, do.

The teacher now exercises the class on the tones of this key in the manner already indicated, and questions about what has been done, and about the lessons to be sung, as follows: *What is the name of this new key? What are the names of its pitches? What is its signature? What clef is here used? What kind of time? When the treble staff is arranged for the key of E, what pitch does the space below stand for? The first space? Second line? Third space? &c.* Name the pitches of the first lesson.

No. 109.—Round.

Do,   do,   do,   mi,   sol, sol, sol,   do, sol, do, sol,   mi, mi, mi.

Pip - ing up so clear and strong; Cuck-oo, Cuck-oo, hear the song.

No. 110.—Round.

Do,   do,   do,   do,   do,   do,   do,   do,   mi,   mi,   mi,   mi,

Now the black-smith's arm is swing - ing, And this cheer - ful

mi,   mi,   mi,   mi,   sol,   sol,   do,   do.

song he's sing - ing, Cling,   cling,   Clang,   clang.

No. 111.

Do,   mi,   mi,   mi,   sol, sol, sol,   do,   si,   la,   sol,   mi,   sol,   do,

1. O   gai - ly   the plow-man his   ox - en   is   call - ing, Gee up,
2. Now down in   the pond all the   frog-gies are   fall - ing, Ker-chunk,

sol,   do,   sol,   do, do, do,   do, do,   mi,   mi,   mi,   sol, sol, sol,

gee up, Haw Bright, now come here; A-round them the dead leaves are
ker-chunk, And splash in   he   starts, And, pop-ping his head up his

do,   si,   la,   sol,   mi,   sol,   do,   sol,   do,   sol,   do,   do,   do,   do.

qui - et - ly   fall - ing; How gay   the   day, How bright and how clear.
speck-led coat flash-ing, Will   cry, Good bye, And   un - der   he   darts.

No. 112.

Do,	si,	la,	sol,	sol,	do,	mi,	sol,	sol,	fa,	re,

1. Bim, bom, bim, bom, Hear them ring - ing loud and clear;
2. Bim, bom, bim, bom, What is it they say to mo?

do,	si,	la,	sol,	sol,	do,	mi,	sol,	fa,	ro,	do.

Bim, bom, bim, bom, Pleas - ing sound to ev - 'ry ear.
Bim, bom, bim, bom, Do your work as well as we.

CHAPTER XX.

All sing our old acquaintance, the scale of C. Now listen while I sing, omitting B, and putting in its place a sound which is between B and A, and which we will call B flat.

The teacher then commences at the upper C, and sings C, B flat, A, G, F. After the class have done the same thing, he says, now let us see what this throwing away B, and substituting B flat, will give us.

After this is ascertained, he says, a character called a FLAT is used to make the degrees of the staff that have stood for B, stand for B flat. The teacher then exercises the class by pointing to the scales represented as below:

No. 113.

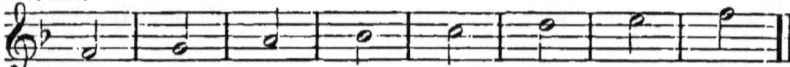

F,	G,	A,	B flat,	C,	D,	E,	F.
1,	2,	3,	4,	5,	6,	7,	8.
Do,	re,	mi,	fa,	sol,	la,	si,	do.

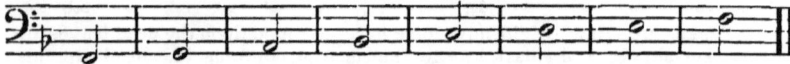

No. 114.

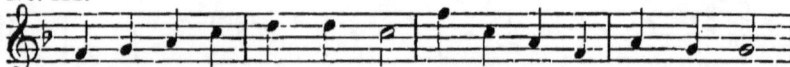

Do,	re,	mi,	sol,	la,	la,	sol,	do,	sol,	mi,	do,	mi,	re,	re,

1. One, two, three, five, up we go; Eight, five, three, one, down a - gain:
2. "Once a - gain," the teach - er says, So once more we sing it through.

Do, re, mi, sol, la, la, sol, do, sol, mi, do, mi, re, do.
Back a - gain un - til we know Ev - 'ry move-ment of the strain.
We will sing our mer - ry lays, 'Till he says that "That will do."

No. 115.

Do, sol, sol, sol, sol, mi, do, re, mi, re, do, do, re, mi, fa.
1. Three cheers for our he-roes, Not those who wear stars, Not those who wear
2. But cheers for our sol-diers, Rough, wrin-kled and brown, The men who make

sol, la, si, do, sol, mi, re, re, sol, sol, sol, sol, fa, mi,
ea - gles, and leaf - lets, and bars; We know they are gal - lant and
he - roes, and ask no re - nown, Un - self - ish, un - tir - ing, in-

fa, fa, sol, la, la, sol, la, si, do, sol, mi, re, mi, re, do.
hon - or them too, For brave-ly main - tain - ing the Red, White and Blue.
trep - id and true, The bul-wark sur-round-ing, the Red, White and Blue.

No. 116.

Do, do, si, si, la, la, sol, fa, fa, mi, fa, sol, sol, do,
1. Now be - neath the key-note we Sing our les - son o'er with glee;
2 We are not quite sure just yet That this one we shan't for - get;

do, do, si, si, la, la, sol, fa, fa, mi, fa, sol, sol, do.
Prac - tice, per - fect makes, they say, May we per - fect be some day.
So, to be con-vinced we shan't, Once a - gain this strain we chant.

CHAPTER XXI.

All sing F, G, A, B flat. Now listen while I sing down, beginning with B flat. I shall omit E, and sing E flat in its stead. The teacher then sings the scale of B flat down. After the class have done the same thing, he says, E flat is one name of the tone that is half way between E and D. We used this same pitch in the key of E, but there it was called D sharp.

After finding the key-note, the usual exercises in singing from pointing to the notes of the scale takes place.

No. 117.

B flat,   C,   D,   E flat,   F,   G,   A,   B flat.
1,   2,   3,   4,   5,   6,   7,   8.
Do,   re,   mi,   fa,   sol,   la,   si,   do.

No. 118.

Do,   re,   mi,   sol,   fa,   mi,   re,   do,   si,   la,   sol,   la,   si,   do,
1. Now, that we have changed the key, We must ver - y   care - ful   be;
2. When he's sure of that, he'll soon Let   us   sing   an - oth - er   tune;

do,   re,   mi,   sol,   fa,   mi,   re,   do,   si,   la,   sol,   fa,   sol,   do.
Let   us make the teach - er   see, We'll not miss the   flat - ted   E.
Com-rades, sing with joy - ful   care, And   of sing - ing wrong be-ware.

No. 119.

Sol,   do,   sol,   do,   mi,   re,   do,   si,   sol,   do,   sol,   mi,   sol,
1. "The   moon   is bright, the   dew   is sweet, The mead - ow pleas - ant
2. "My   moth - er   al - ways says, 'tis best To stud - y   first   and

do, mi, re, sol,   do, sol, do, mi, re, do, si, sol,
to   our feet; Come let   us   roam a   lit - tle way, We
play for rest; So   let   us   go   to   school, and then We'll

la, si, do, mi, re, re, do, re, re, si, sol, do, re, mi, do,
will not go to school to - day.'' This a lit - tle boy did say To
like our plays as much a-gain.'' Don't you think that boy was wise, Who

re, re, si, sol,   do, mi, re, sol,   do, sol, do, mi,
one who was with him   at   play; But   sing the com - ing
did the oth - er thus ad - vise? And if   you do,   I

re, do, si, sol,   la, si, do, mi,   ro, re,   do.
verse, and see What his wise friend's ad - vice will be.
hope you'll take His   mot - to, for your teach - er's sake.

No. 120.—Round. *(In two parts.)*

1   [*The second section commences when the first reaches the first heavy bar.*]

Do, do, do, do,   do, si, sol, la   si, do, re, mi,
Come, broth - ers, come, the mer - ry tune is   sound - ing;

2

mi, mi, mi, mi, sol, fa, mi, re, mi, fa, fa, mi, do.
Come, join our cheer - ful song, with joy each heart is bound - ing.

(The teacher will explain at the proper time that the pause ⌢ indicates that the tone is to be prolonged beyond its usual time.)

4

CHAPTER XXII.

All sing the scale of B flat. Now listen while I sing, and name each pitch as I give it. I will begin at the upper B flat, and think that perhaps you can tell the name of the new pitch that I introduce, and also the name of the key-note that results from its use. The teacher then sings B flat, A flat, G, F and E flat. After the class have named the pitches, and have sung them, and have also ascertained the key-note, the usual exercise in the scale takes place.

No. 121.

E flat,	F,	G,	A flat,	B flat,	C,	D,	E flat.
1,	2,	3,	4,	5,	6,	7,	8.
Do,	re,	mi,	fa,	sol,	la,	si,	do.

No. 122.

Sol, sol, do, sol, sol, mi, do, mi, sol, do, si, la, sol,

1. Up, up, up, down, down, down, One, three, five, eight, seven, six, five;
2. Is it not ver - y kind, That our teach - er takes such care;

sol, sol, do, sol, sol, mi, do, re, mi, fa, mi, re, do.

Mer - ry we not a frown, While to con - quer this we strive
Let us all try to mind What he says a - bout this air.

No. 123.—ROUND. [*Each section commences when the preceding one reaches the first heavy bar.*]

Sol, mi, do, mi, sol, la, sol, mi, do, mi, sol, do, do.

There was a lit - tle lamb - kin, Whose fleece was ver - y white.

No. 124.

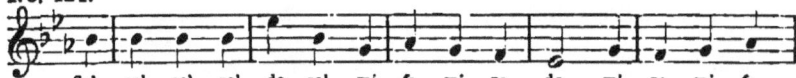

Sol, sol, sol, sol, do, sol, mi, fa, mi, re, do, mi, re, mi, fa,

1. God bless the brave sail-or, who rides o'er the main, And bat - tles with
2. Oh fill his sails, fill his sails, soft breath-ing wind, O car - ry him

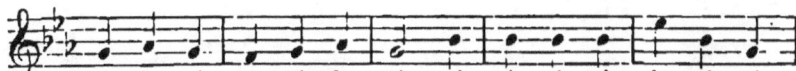

mi, fa, mi, re, mi, fa, mi, sol, sol, sol, sol, do, sol, mi,

ma - ny a ter - ri - ble gale; His hard-ships are ma - ny, yet
safe o'er the treach-er - ous main; And leav - ing all storm and all

fa, mi, re, do, mi, re, mi, fa, mi, fa, sol, la, do, si, do.

ev - er the same, He loves o'er the dark, blue sea - wa - ter to sail.
dan-ger be - hind, Just waft him a - long to his dear home a - gain.

No. 125.

Do, do, do, do, do, do, mi, sol, mi, do, si, la, si, do,

1. Our teach - er thinks it best we should go down be - low the key,
2. For, if he did not think we ought, we may be ver - y sure

mi, mi, sol, fa, mi, re, mi, fa, re, si, sol, la, si, do.

And up a - bove as well, so let us all o - be - dient be.
He'd not have let us do it, but have told us so be - fore.

CHAPTER XXIII.

All sing the scale of E flat. Now sing the lower E flat again, but instead of applying the syllable *do* to it, sing *sol*, and think of it as five—sing it again—again. Now sing the next pitch above, which is F, but consider it six, and sing *la*—again, once more, now five, six, seven, eight, seven, six, five, four—four again. You are now singing a new pitch, it is not D, the one you have been singing next below E flat, but it is D flat; and if we keep on down to one, we shall find out what key the addition of D flat makes. All sing the E flat, or five, again, now four, three, two, one. Now I will sing, beginning with the E flat, and you may name each pitch as I give it.

The teacher then sings E flat, D flat, C, B flat and A flat. *What is the key-note?*

No. 126.

A flat,	B flat,	C,	D flat,	E flat,	F,	G,	A flat.
1,	2,	3,	4,	5,	6,	7,	8.
Do,	re,	mi,	fa,	sol,	la,	si,	do.

No. 127.

| Do, | do, | do, | do, | do, | si, | la, | sol, | la, | si, | do, |

1. A flat,   A flat, Let us all re - mem - ber that;
2. Once more, once more, Sing it bet - ter than be - fore;

| ro, | re, | si, | sol, | la, | si, | do, | si, | sol, | la, | si, | do, | do, | do. |

For it will be ver - y well That the key-note we can tell.
For if we our sing-ing love, We are cer-tain to im - prove.

No. 128.

| Sol, | do, | do, | do, | si, | re, | sol, | do, | do, | do, | si, | re, |

1. The voice of the morn - ing is call - ing to child-hood,
  And Ma - ry, the love --li - est nymph of the wild wood,
D. C. From glance and from smile there beams some-thing e - lys - ian,

2. Yet, oh! to her heart moth - er Na - ture hath giv - en
  She loves ev - 'ry star that sheds ra - diance in heav - en,
D. C. But dews that like tears on the lil - ies are trem-bling,

FINE.

sol, mi, re, do, si, la, sol, la, la, si, do,

From stream - let, and val - ley, and moun - tain it calls; }
Is cross - ing the brook where the mill wa - ter falls: }
She has but one fail - ing—sweet Ma - ry is poor.
The kind - est af - fec - tions that mor - tal can know; }
And al - so the flow - ers as God's im - age below: }
Are types but of Ma - ry— for Ma - ry is poor.

mi, re, re, mi, do, sol, mi, re, re, mi, do, sol,

Oh! love - ly is Ma - ry, her face like a vi - sion,
'Tis pit - y to think that a be - ing re - sem - bling

D. C.

sol, do, re, do, si, do, si, la, si, la, sol.

Once seen leaves a charm that will ev - er en - dure;
The fair - est in beau - ty, such lot should en - dure;

No. 129.—Round. (*In four parts.*)

Do, mi, re, sol, la, do, si, do, mi, re, do,

Let us sing an - oth - er gay Round, Join in, com-

si, re, sol, fa, mi, fa, mi, do, sol, do, sol,

pan - ions, to swell the glad sound; Come, come, let each

do, mi, sol, sol, sol, sol, la, la, sol, do.

young heart bound, Glad, glad to join in our Round.

CHAPTER XXIV.

All sing four measures—double time, quarter notes, pitch G, syllable *la*.

Now again, but instead of singing one sound to each beat, sing two. When this is well done, the teacher says, these are EIGHTH NOTES, and would be represented thus:

No. 130.

La, la, la, la, la, la, la, la, la, la, la, la, la, la, la, la.

Now four triple measures of eighth notes—same pitch, same syllable.

Now four quadruple measures of eighth notes—same pitch, same syllable

Now four sextuple measures in the same way.

It will be observed, that one dash at the end of the quarter note makes an eighth note, whether on one alone, or joining two or more together. The following are all eighth notes, having the same length:

No. 131.

La, la, la, la, la, la, la, la, la, la, la, la, la, la, la, la.

There is no need now of printing the syllables, but they should be sung before the other words are applied. Name the pitches of the lesson before singing.

No. 132.

Now beat the time, and let the eighth notes ring; Don't make the

mo-tions fast - er than you sing, Tra, la, la, la, la, la, la, la, la.

No. 133.

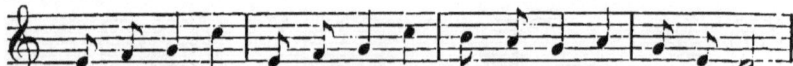

1. Blow, ye breez-es! sum-mer greets you, With her soft and ten-der heat;
2. Sweet-ly are her show-ers fall-ing, From the foun-tain far on high;

Now her fair - y fin - ger meets you, Now her swell-ing puls - es beat
And the mer - ry birds are call - ing, As they roam the west-ern sky

No. 134.

1. There is mu - sic on the wa - ters, As they on-ward ev - er flow,
2. There is mu - sic by the foun-tain, Where the wa-ters bub-ble o'er,
3. There is mu - sic to the wea - ry, Where the wa-ters of their soul

Thro' the pleas-ant plains and val-leys, Where the rose and lil - ies grow.
Like the last link of a spir - it, Bound to earth by sin no more.
Cease on earth to flow for - ev - er, And in heav - en find their goal.

CHAPTER XXV.

Hitherto the quarter note has been the standard, or the one to fill one part of any measure (or one beat). In double measure it has taken two quarters (or their value) to fill each measure—in triplets, three, &c. There is no particular reason why this should be so—the eighth may be the standard if we choose to have it so, or the half. The following song sounds the *same* in its three representations, although it looks so differently. In the first, an eighth, or the value of an eighth, fills each part of the measure, a quarter requiring two beats, &c. In the second, a quarter fills each part, as heretofore; and in the third, a half. It may seem strange that a half should be used in one piece to stand for the same length that a quarter does in another, or an eighth in another; but this will serve to show that notes have no *positive* value, only *relative*. It will, however, be observed that in the *same piece* the quarter is twice as long as the eighth, and half as long as the half, &c.

No. 135.

Let us re - mem - ber when we roam, The friends we leave be - hind;)
And let our tho'ts go forth to them, In feel - ings pure and kind. (

Let us re - mem - ber when we roam, The friends we leave be - hind:)
And let our tho'ts go forth to them, In feel - ings pure and kind. (

Let us re - mem - ber when we roam, The friends we leave be - hind; ⎰
And let our tho'ts go forth to them, In feel - ings pure and kind. ⎱

It now becomes necessary to have some way of indicating which kind of note is taken as the standard. This is done by figures—2 stands for a half note, 4 for a quarter, 8 for an eighth, &c. The figure 2 also stands for double measure, 3 for triple, 4 for quadruple, and 6 for sextuple, and so are also used to indicate the kind of time or measure.

Two figures are, therefore, usually placed at the commencement of a piece of music in the form of a fraction—the upper to show what kind of time is made use of, and the lower what kind of a note (or its value) is to occur on each part of the measure or beat; thus: $\frac{2}{2}$ shows double measure with a half (or its value) to each beat; or, in other words, two half notes (or their value) in each measure.

This is said to be HALF VARIETY of double time. Quarter variety of double time would be indicated by $\frac{2}{4}$, eighth variety by $\frac{2}{8}$, half variety of triple time by $\frac{3}{2}$, &c.

We can have as many varieties of measure as there are kinds of notes, but the three already mentioned (half, quarter and eighth) are the only ones in common use.

When two figures are placed at the commencement of a piece of music, what is the upper one for? What the lower? What would the figures $\frac{4}{2}$ stand for? (Ans. Quadruple measure, half variety.) How many half notes in a measure? How many quarters? What kind of a note to each beat? How many varieties of measure could we have? How many are in common use? What are they? In what kind of time is the following song written? Which variety? If an eighth occupies one beat, what kind of a note will take two beats? What three? (Ans. DOTTED QUARTER NOTE.) How many eighths is a dotted quarter equal to?

It will be an excellent plan in the following songs, to name, first the tones that make the key, then give the scale names of the tones that make the lesson, and then sing syllables.

No. 136.
ALLEGRETTO   FINE.

1. A - wake thee, lit - tle sleep - er,   No lon - ger slum-b'ring lie, ⎱
     The ro - sy light is break - ing   O'er all the East - ern sky; ⎰
D. C. While all the air is ring - ing   With sweet-est mel - o - dy.
2. A - wake thee, lit - tle sleep - er,   And view the glo-rious sun, ⎱
     His cir - cuit thro' the heav - ens   Al - rea - dy is be - gun; ⎰
D. C. Then hast - ens on his jour - ney   Far o - ver vale and hill.
3. Be - hold him as he speed-eth   Up - on his on-ward way, ⎱
     For nev - er once he paus - eth   'Till even - ing's clos - ing ray; ⎰
D. C. So shall thy rest be glo-rious,   When life has pass'd a - way.

D. C.

And joy - ous birds are wing - ing Their flight from tree to tree,
He looks in at thy win - dow, To find thee sleep - ing still;
Thus let thy path be on - ward And up - ward ev - 'ry day;

In the following song there are six eighths (or their value) in a measure. It is more convenient to beat this in double time than in sextuple, because the sextuple beats would be so quick. Make three eighths (or their value) to a beat. There may be some difficulty in starting. The lesson begins on the last part of the upward beat. Question about key, &c. (It may, perhaps, be well before singing this to practice beating double measure, and singing three eighths, or a quarter and eighth to a beat, pitch G, syllable *la*.)

No. 137.

1. Shall we stand still? Oh no, oh no; Go on-ward ev-'ry one!
2. In work or play, what-e'er we do, Re-mem-ber this each one;

The mot-to is, still on-ward go, Go on, go on, go on!
Those must, who would in good-ness grow, Go on, go on, go on!

Go on, go on, go on, go on, The mot-to is, Go on.
Go on, go on, go on, go on, The mot-to is, Go on.

An EIGHTH REST is like a quarter rest, only turned the other way—something like the figure 7. Before singing the next song, it may be well to practice lessons like the following, to learn to come in on the last part of a beat.

No. 138.

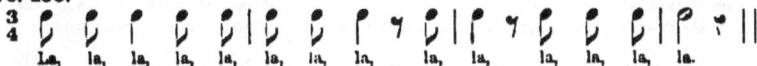

La, la, la, la, la, la, la, la, la, la, la, la, la, la.

Question about key, kind of time, variety, &c. Name tones of key (pitch names), names of lesson (scale names), then sing with syllables.

No. 139.

1. There is a child, a boy or girl, I'm sor-ry it is true,
2. I know a child, a boy or girl, I'm loth to say I do,
3. I know a child, a boy or girl, I hope that such are few,
4. A girl there is, a girl I know, and I could love her too;

Who does not mind when spo-ken to; Is that— can that be you?
Who struck a lit - tle play-mate hard; Is that— can that be you?
Who told a lie, yes, told a lie; Is that— can that be you?
But that she is so proud and vain; Is that— can that be you?

Question about kind of time, variety, key, signature, &c.

No. 140.—Round. (*In three parts.*)

To each beat a half note sing; Twice as fast, or two to one, the

quar-ters next we bring; Now both to - geth - er hear them ring.

CHAPTER XXVI.

All sing four measures in double time, one sound to each beat, pitch G, syllable *la.* This we could represent by quarters, halves or eighths. We will take half notes:

No. 141.

Now again, but let there be two notes to the second beat of each measure. *If a half note is taken as the standard, what kind of notes would these be?* This would be represented thus:

No. 142.

Now again, and connect the first and second notes in each measure into one, thus:

No. 143.

This is difficult, and to beat and sing, will require to be practiced some time. Alternating by teacher and class is a good way to practice.

Before singing the next song, it will be a good plan to practice exercises like the following, to prepare for the note which occupies a beat and a half:

No. 144.

It will be remembered, that in beating time *well*, the motion is made quickly, and the hand rests at the end of the beat until the time of the beat, or part of measure, has expired; so the sound that is a half a beat long is made *after* the motion, and while the hand is waiting at its point of rest.

Question about key, signature, kind of time, variety, and sing first with syllables.

No. 145.

1. How thor-ough-ly and si - lent - ly The sun per-forms its du - ty,
2. Each morn-ing when it ris - es up, And peeps a - bove the bush-es;
3. The lark, from out her earth - y bed, Flies,sing-ing, up to heav-en;
4. And shall we more un-grate-ful be Than are the lark and flow-ers?

Of call - ing up from all the earth The flow - er forms of beau-ty.
The flow - ers take a sud - den start From in a - mong the rush - es.
Her song of praise for one more day, Which has to her been giv - en.
No, we will all give ear - nest thanks For all our hap - py hours.

CHAPTER XXVII.

All sing two measures in quadruple time, pitch G, syllable *la*, one sound to a beat. Suppose these to be quarter notes. Now sing two measures again, but this time fill them with eighth notes—two to a beat.

Now again, and sing three notes to each beat. After this is practiced until it can be well done, the teacher says, this would be represented by eighth notes grouped in threes, with the figure **3** over them, thus:

No. 146.

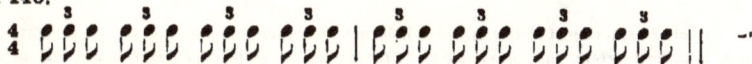

No. 147.—Round. (*In three parts.*)

Sing mer - ri - ly, sing, for the sum - mer time is com - ing;

Sing mer - ri - ly, sing, for the sum - mer time is com - ing;

Mer-ri-ly, mer-ri-ly, mer-ri-ly, mer-ri-ly, mer-ri-ly, mer-ri-ly, mer-ri-ly, mer-ri-ly.

These groups are called TRIPLETS.

Now sing two measures again in quadruple time, pitch G, syllable *la*, one sound to a beat.

Now again, with two sounds to each beat.

Now again, but with three sounds to each beat.

Now again, but with four sounds to each beat. When this is done neatly and distinctly, the teacher says, if we have a quarter note as our standard, four sounds to a beat will be represented by SIXTEENTH NOTES, thus:

No. 148.

Sing two measures again, making an eighth and two sixteenths to each beat. That would be represented thus:

No. 149.

When this is well done, the teacher says, now join the first and second note of each beat (eighth and sixteenth) into one sound. That would be represented thus:

No. 150.

You observe, that just as the dotted whole note is equal to three half notes, the dotted half note to three quarters, the dotted quarter to three eighths, so the dotted eighth is equal to three sixteenths. Please practice these groupings in the different kinds of time. It is not very difficult.

No. 151.

See the lit - tle brook - let how it dan - ces o'er the lea,

Ev - er sing - ing cheer - ful - ly its qui - et mel - o - dy;

Leap - ing up to kiss the flow'rs that bloom a - long its way,

Hap - py, use - ful lit - tle brook, I love by thee to stray.

If you beat double time in the next song, it amounts to a kind of triplet to each beat, with occasionally a dotted eighth and sixteenth instead of even eighths. This kind of music is not hard to sing, although it looks somewhat formidable.

No. 152.

1. The   ta - ble was set, and the tea - ket - tle sang, By the
2. They wait - ed for fa - ther. So, night af - ter night, They had
3. O, who is it comes in the dark - ness and rain, To the

fire - side pleas-ant and snug; The voice of the crick-et in
watch'd as the year had gone by, For his face at the door,'till the
farm on the brow of the hill? And who is it peeps thro'the

mer - ri - ment rang, And puss lay a - sleep on the rug.
tear-drops were bright In the deeps of each play-wea - ry eye.
glim - mer - ing pane, At the group that is joy - less and still?

The rain　on　the　win - dow - sill tapp'd with　a　will,　As　the
Ah!　slow　were　the　steps　of　the　hours　that pass'd,　Tho' when
A　hand　on　the　latch, and　a　voice loud and clear, Then　a

moth - er look'd out　in　the　gloom;　And　three lit - tle chil-dren were
even-ing grew chill - y　and　long,　And the arms of the wind round the
form by　the door stands in view!　O,　moth-er and chil-dren, dash

sit - ting so　still, In　the　shade　of　the　dim - light - ed　room.
old house were cast,Still the　crick - et breathed hope in　her　song.
by　ev - 'ry tear—Clasp your sol - dier,　so　no - ble and　true!

Name key, kind of time, variety, pitches, and sing—first with syllables.

No. 153.

ANDANTE.

1. Once in spring a　lit - tle　flow - er Pushed its　head　up thro' the
2. First the leaves look'd ver-y　yel - low,　But they slow - ly turn'd to
3. Then a　bud　made its　ap - pear-ance,Slow - ly burst in - to　a

earth, Peep'd a - bout　and　went　on　grow - ing,　Ris - ing
green; And the　flow'r grew tall - er,　strong - er,　As　the
flow'r; Then the　rain came　and　the　dew　fell,　Soft - ly

slow - ly from　the　earth, From the　spot　that gave　it　birth.
leaves be - came more green　Than they, days　be - fore, had been.
kiss - ing,　and　the　flow'r Fresh - er look'd for　ev - 'ry show'r.

No. 154.

1. Weep for the fall-en, hang your head in sor-row, And
2. Voi-ces of wail-ing tell of hope-less an-guish, While
3. Hark! how they bid us sound the time-ly warn-ing, While
4. Weep for the fall-en; but in all your sor-row, Point

mourn-ful-ly sing the re-quiem sad and slow; Thousands have perished
sor-row-ing moth-ers bid us on-ward go; Hark! to the ac-cents
yet there is hope to shun the cup of woe; For is it noth-ing
all to the pledge, *that* free-dom can be-stow, Res-cue the na-tion

by the fell de-stroy-er; O! weep for youth and beau-ty in the grave laid low.
of the broken hearted, Who weep for youth and beau-ty in the grave laid low.
ye, who see no dan-ger, To weep for youth and beau-ty in the grave laid low?
from the fell de-stroy-er; O! *why* should youth and beau-ty in the grave lay low?

No. 155.

1. Take the pledge! take the pledge! The temp'rance banner view; Take the
2. Take the pledge! take the pledge! The balm for many a wound; Take the
3. Take the pledge! take the pledge! Here comes the conqu'ring host; Take tho

pledge! take the pledge! And then your course pursue; March bold-ly on! the
pledge! take the pledge! A glo-rious prize is found; March bold-ly on! and
pledge! take the pledge! No more of sin we boast; March bold-ly on! and

vic-t'ry now has come; March bold-ly on! a might-y con-quest's won.
bend your might-y bow; March bold-ly on! and lay th' in-vad-er low.
let your ban-ners fly: March bold-ly on! and con-quer, tho' you die.

CHAPTER XXVIII.

There are other keys in music beside those we have now passed through, but they are so little used in singing, that we will only introduce them enough to sing the scales that belong to them.

The key of B is made of the tones B, C sharp, D sharp, E, F sharp, G sharp and A sharp.

The key of F sharp is made of the tones F sharp, G sharp, A sharp, B, C sharp, D sharp and E sharp.

The key of G flat is the same in sound as the key of F sharp, but the tones are named differently. They are G flat, A flat, B flat, C flat, D flat, E flat and F.

The key of D flat is made of the tones D flat, E flat, F, G flat, A flat, B flat and C.

It will be a pleasant exercise to sing in order the scales of all the keys that have been introduced. This is called TRANSPOSING by fifths, because each successive scale begins on what was five of the previous one. You will notice in this transposition, that one sharp is added at each new key, or that one flat is taken away, excepting at the key of G flat, which is the same in sound as the key of F sharp.

The change from the scale of F sharp to that of G flat is said to be an ENHARMONIC change. It will be a good plan to make the singing of the scales a daily exercise for the present. Learn to sing them without an instrument—going directly from each to the next in perfect time.

No 156.

Do, re, mi, fa, sol, la, si,   do, si, la, sol, fa, mi, re,   do, mi, sol, do, sol, mi, · do.

Do, re, mi, fa, sol, la, si,   do, si, la, sol, fa, mi, re,   do, mi, sol, do, sol, mi,   do.

Do, re, mi, fa, sol, la, si,   do, si, la, sol, fa, mi, re,   do, mi, sol, do, sol, mi,   do.

Do, re, mi, fa, sol, la, si,   do, si, la, sol, fa, mi, re,   do, mi, sol, do, sol, mi,   do.

Do, re, mi, fa, sol, la, si,   do, si, la, sol, fa, mi, re,   do, mi, sol, do, sol, mi,   do.

Do, re, mi, fa, sol, la, si, do, si, la, sol, fa, mi, re, do, mi, sol, do, sol, mi, do.

Do, re, mi, fa, sol, la, si, do, si, la, sol, fa, mi, re, do, mi, sol, do, sol, mi, do.

Do, re, mi, fa, sol, la, si, do, si, la, sol, fa, mi, re, do, mi, sol, do, sol, mi do.

Do, re, mi, fa, sol, la, si, do, si, la, sol, fa, mi, re, do, mi, sol. do, sol, mi, do.

Do, re, mi, fa, sol, la, si, do, si, la, sol, fa, mi, re, do, mi, sol, do, sol, mi, do.

Do, re, mi, fa, sol, la, si, do, si, la, sol, fa, mi, re, do, mi, sol, do, sol, mi, do.

Do, re, mi, fa, sol, la, si, do, si, la, sol, fa, mi, re, do, mi, sol, do, sol, mi, do.

Do, re, mi, fa, sol, la, si, do, si, la, sol, fa, mi, re, do, mi, sol, do, sol, mi, do.

Do, re, mi, fa, sol, la, si, do, si, la, sol, fa, mi, re, do, mi, sol, do, sol, mi, do.

CHAPTER XXIX.

The teacher gives two pitches an octave apart. After the class have done the same thing, the teacher says, the difference in pitch between any two tones is, in music, called an INTERVAL. All give this interval of an octave again. Now observe whether I give a larger or smaller interval than this. Teacher sings *one* and *seven*. After they have answered, he gives *one* and *six*, then *one* and *five*, and so on down to *one* and *two*. All sing *one* and *two* This is the smallest interval yet, and is called a STEP. Now listen again. Teacher sings *one* and *sharp one*, or *flat two*. All do the same. This is the smallest interval used in music, and is called a HALF STEP. All sing G. Now a step above it. Now G again. Now a half step above it. After practicing steps and half steps from various tones of the scale, the teacher says, in the scales the tones seem to succeed each other with the same interval; but the fact is, that between *three* and *four* and between *seven* and *eight* the intervals are but half steps, while in all the other cases they are steps. Sing the scale again carefully, and see if you can perceive this fact. *What is the interval caused by one and two? Two and three? Three and four? Four and five? Five and six? Six and seven? Seven and eight?*

CHAPTER XXX.

Hitherto in each piece that has been sung, only one key has been used; but it is pleasant sometimes to change the key *during* a song, and this is frequently done (always returning to the first key to end with). This is, of course, accomplished by introducing the peculiar tone of the new key; as, for example, if we are singing in the key of C, introducing the tone F sharp instead of F, will make us sing in the key of G, and then introducing the F again will bring us back to C.

Going from one key to another during a piece of music is called MODULATION.

Modulation is accomplished by changing the signification of the staff somewhere in the tune, instead of at the beginning.

When the sharps and flats are used for this purpose, they are called ACCIDENTALS.

The effect of an accidental continues only through the measure in which it occurs.

This rule has but one exception, viz: when the last note of the measure is on the degree of the staff affected by the accidental, and the first note of the next measure is on the same degree, its effect is continued through that measure also—thus making it possible to continue the effect of an accidental through many measures.

No. 157.

Mi, mi, mi, re, mi, sol, fa, re, re, re, sol, fa, mi,
1. Now our la - bors are end - ing, Free from toil of the day;
2. Who, when dark-ness a - round us Seals our eye-lids in sleep,

sol, sol, fi, mi, fi, sol, la, si, do, si, la, mi, fi,

Here our voi - ces all blend - ing, Drive we all sor - row a-
Who, when slum - ber hath bound us, All our young spir - its will

sol, la, sol, fa, mi, re, mi, fa, sol, fa, re, do.

way: Peace-ful even - ing Fol - low - eth now the glad day.
keep? Ho - ly an - gels Kind - ly will watch o'er our sleep!

What key beside the key of C is introduced into this lesson ? At which measure does the modulation take place? By what pitch does the modulation take place ? In how many measures do we feel that we are in the key of G ? By what pitch do we return to the key of C?

(In modulation, the syllables may be changed to the new key, if the teacher thinks best; it is not, however, very important.)

No. 158.

Do, mi, sol, sol, la, la, sol, se, se, la, la, do,

1. Night has spread her sa - ble pall O - ver all the earth;
2. Birds, and flow'rs, and hum-ming bees, Rest in slum - ber light;
3. Slum - ber light thro' all the night, Tinged with hap - py dreams;

do, mi, sol, sol, la, la, sol, la, la, si, si, do.

Hushed are sounds of bu - sy toil, Hushed the songs of mirth.
And as we our couch - es seek, Bid we all good night.
May our guar - dian keep us all, 'Till the morn - ing beams.

What key is introduced into this lesson ? What tone belongs to the key of F that does not belong to the key of C? What tone belongs to the key C that does not belong to the key of F? How far does the effect of the accidental continue in this song ? To which department in music do intervals belong ? To which do steps and half steps belong ? To which modulation ? What would be the note of modulation ? What would be the note of modulation in going from the key of G to the key of D, or what tone belongs to the key of D that does not belong to the key of G? What would be the note of modulation in going from the key of F to the key of B flat ? &c.

CHAPTER XXXI.

A tone not belonging to a key may be introduced, and passed over so quickly as not to give the impression of a change of key.

No. 159.

Sol, fi, sol, do,   mi, ri. mi, sol,   do, re, mi, sol,   fa, mi, re,
1. How de-light-ful,   a - ged win-ter,   Are thy brac-ing winds to me;
2. Clad in snow-flakes caught de-scend-ing, And   to   keep them from the sun;

sol, fi, sol, do,   mi, ri, mi, sol,   do, re, mi, sol,   fa, re, do,
Thro' the keen air   on your pin-ions Throng a troop   in wild-est glee;
Round-ing cor-ners 'mid the shad-ows, 'Till "old sol" his   race had run,

la, si, la, do,   sol, fi, sol, do,   si, la, sol, fa,   mi, re, do.
In   the moon-light by   the stream-let Elfs of frost-y   land I   see.
Ev - er   rea - dy when sweet Lu - na   Ran-soms them a - gain for   fun.

It is sometimes desirable to restore a line or space already modified by a flat or a sharp to its original signification before the measure ends. A character called a NATURAL is made use of for this purpose. A natural is also an accidental.

No. 160.

Sol, fi, fa,   mi, sol, fi,   fa, mi,   sol, sol, sol, la, se, si, do.
Gen-tly a - long Float-eth the song Of the low mur-mur-ing rill.

Such accidental tones as do not produce the impression of a change of key, are called CHRO-MATIC tones.

Taking any key, and putting in all the chromatic tones, gives us the CHROMATIC SCALE. The scale we have already sung is called the DIATONIC SCALE.

No. 161.—CHROMATIC SCALE. *Key of C.*

Do,	di,	re,	ri,	mi,	fa,	fi,	sol	si,	la,	li,	si,	do,
1,	sharp 1,	2,	sharp 2,	3,	4,	sharp 4,	5,	sharp 5	6	sharp 6,	7,	8.

do,	si,	se,	la,	le,	sol,	se,	fa,	mi,	me,	re,	ra,	do.
8,	7,	flat 7,	6,	flat 6,	5,	flat 5,	4,	3,	flat-3,	2,	flat 2,	1.

No. 162. CHROMATIC SCALE. *Key of D.*

Do,	di,	re,	ri,	mi,	fa,	fi,	sol,	si,	la,	li,	si,	do,
1,	sharp 1,	2,	sharp 2,	3,	4,	sharp 4,	5,	sharp 5,	6,	sharp 6,	7,	8,

do,	si,	se,	la,	le,	sol,	se,	fa,	mi,	me,	re,	ra,	do.
8,	7,	flat 7,	6,	flat 6,	5,	flat 5,	4,	3,	flat 3,	2,	flat 2,	1.

No. 163. CHROMATIC SCALE. *Key of F.*

Do,	di,	re,	ri,	mi,	fa,	fi,	sol,	si,	la,	li,	si,	do,
1,	sharp 1,	2,	sharp 2,	3,	4,	sharp 4,	5,	sharp 5,	6,	sharp 6,	7,	8,

do,	si,	se,	la,	le,	sol,	se,	fa,	mi,	me,	re,	ra,	do.
8,	7,	flat 7,	6,	flat 6,	5,	sharp 4,	4,	3,	flat 3,	2,	flat 2,	1.

How many kinds of intervals are there in the chromatic scale? What is it?

CHAPTER XXXII.

Sometimes it is desirable to sing two or more sounds to one syllable. The notes to be so sung are connected by a character like the tie, but called a LEGATO MARK. It will be an excellent plan here to practice the scale, giving two of its pitches to one syllable, ascending and descending, after which the following song:

No. 164.

ALLEGRETTO.

Mi, fa, fi, sol, la, sol, mi, fa, fi, sol, sol, la, la, la,

1. Breath-ing so soft - ly a - long the gay mead, The spring time is
2. Flow'r-ets a - wake in the sweet ver-nal air, And fling their new

si, si, si, do.............. mi, fa, fi, sol, la, sol,

com - ing a - gain;...... Laugh - ing rills dance on the
o - dors a - round;...... Song - birds re - turn - ing from

mi, fa, fi, sol, sol, la, la, la, si, si, si, do.........

hill - side a - bove, And mur - mur a - way on the plain.
far dis - tant climes, With joy make the wood-lands re - sound.

You perceive that the F sharp in the foregoing song does not produce the feeling of a change of key, therefore it is regarded as a chromatic tone. In the following song the first sharp does produce the impression of a change of key, but the second does not. *To what key is the modulation? What is the name of the character that connects two notes of different pitch, when they are to be sung to one syllable? What is the name of the same character when it is used to connect two notes of the same pitch?* Name the key, kind of time, and variety of time. Give scale names and pitch names before singing.

No. 165.

Mi, re, do, do, si, do. re...... re, do, si, la, sol,

1. When in the au - tumn the har - vests stand, Wait - ing the
2. When from the for - est the crim - son leaves Float a - way
3. Life, that is on - ly a fleet - ing breath, Soon shall be
4. Fresh as the flow'rs of the ma - ple bough, Bloom - ing and

sol,   ñ,   sol,   la......   la,   sol,   · mi,   fa,   mi,   re,   di,   re,

stroke of the reap - er's hand; Sweet in the sun-shine they
down by the fall - ing sheaves,Sing - ing a mel - o - dy,
bound in the sheaves of death; Live ye through time's sun - ny
gor - ge - ous are ye now; Glad-den the earth as the

mi...... la,   sol,   sol,   la......   do,   si,   sol,   sol,   sol......   si,   do.

smile to know Their work is done; and they glad - ly go.
faint and low, Their work is done; and they glad - ly go.
sum - mer, so, When He shall call, ye may glad - ly go.
flow'rs do, so, When win - ter comes, ye may glad - ly go.

CHAPTER XXXIII.

Take away five in either of the keys that we have been using, and substitute a tone a half step higher, and a great change will be made; not only another key will be the result, but it will be a key of a different kind, more sad and mournful. For example, take out G from the tones that make the key of C, and put G sharp in its place, and you have a key of this kind.

It is called a MINOR KEY.

The keys we have been using are called MAJOR KEYS. (There are no chromatic keys—chromatic tones may come into major and minor keys.)

Here is a song in this minor key that is made of the tones A, B, C, D, E, F and G sharp. See if you can tell by the sound what the key-note is.

No. 166.

Do, re, mi, fa, mi, la, si, la, si, la, mi, re, do, re, mi, fa,

1. Sad - ly a - round us the au-tumn leaves fall, While the dark clouds hang a-
2. Deep in the for - est the gloom-y winds sigh, Bird songs and flow-ers no

mi, re, do, si, la, si, do, re, mi, fa, mi, mi, si, la.

love like a pall, Si-lence and gloom they are spread-ing o'er all.
lon - ger are nigh, Sum-mer, sweet sum-mer, we bid thee good - bye.

The tones of the different minor keys put into scales are as follows.

(We will make use here of the harmonic minor scale only. There are others, but this is the best.)

When it becomes necessary to make a degree of the staff already affected by a sharp stand for a pitch still a half step higher, a character called a DOUBLE SHARP is used. It is first used in the scale of G sharp minor in the following scales.

No. 167.

A minor.

1, 2, 3, 4, 5, 6, 7, 8, 7, 6, 5, 4, 3, 2, 1, 3, 5, 8, 5, 3, 1.
La, si, do, re, mi, fa, si, la, si, fa, mi, re, do, si, la, do, mi, la, mi, do, la.

E minor.

1, 2, 3, 4, 5, 6, 7, 8, 7, 6, 5, 4, 3, 2, 1, 3, 5, 8, 5, 3, 1.
La, si, do, re, mi, fa, si, la, si, fa, mi, re, do, si, la, do, mi, la, mi, do, la.

B minor.

1, 2, 3, 4, 5, 6, 7, 8, 7, 6, 5, 4, 3, 2, 1, 3, 5, 8, 5, 3, 1.
La, si, do, re, mi, fa, si, la, si, fa, mi, re, do, si, la, do, mi, la, mi, do, la.

F sharp minor.

La, si, do, re, mi, fa, si, la, si, fa, mi, re, do, si, la, do, mi, la, mi, do, la.

C sharp minor.

La, si, do, re, mi, fa, si, la, si, fa, mi, re, do, si, la, do, mi, la, mi, do, la.

G sharp minor.

La, si, do, re, mi, fa, si, la, si, fa, mi, re, do, si, la, do, mi, la, mi do, la.

D sharp minor.

La, si, do, re, mi, fa, si, la, si, fa, mi, re, do, si, la, do, mi, la, mi, do, la.

E flat minor.

La, si, do, re, mi, fa, si, la, si, fa, mi, re, do, si, la, do, mi, la, mi, do, la.

B flat minor.

La, si, do, re, mi, fa, si, la, si, fa, mi, re, do, si, la, do, mi,' la, mi, do, la.

F minor.

La, si, do, re, mi, fa, si, la, si, fa, mi, re, do, si, la, do, mi, la, mi, do, la.

C minor.

La, si, do, re, mi, fa, si, la, si, fa, mi, re, do, si, la, do, mi, la, mi, do, la.

G minor.

La, si, do, re, mi, fa, si, la, si, fa, mi, re, do, si, la, do, mi, la, mi, do, la.

D minor.

La, si, do, re, mi, fa, si, la, si, fa, mi, re, do, si, la, do, mi, la, mi, do, la.

A minor.

La, si, do, re, mi, fa, si, la, si, fa, mi, re, do, si, la, do, mi, la, mi, do, la.

You perceive that G sharp, which is one of the tones of this key, is represented by an accidental, and not in the signature. One reason for this is, that relative keys may have the same signature; another is, that another kind of minor scale has G in it as well as G sharp.

You have probably discovered, that the key-note here is A.

The key of A minor is said to be the relative minor to the key of C major.

Every major key has its relative minor, and every minor its relative major.

That which is six in a major key is one in its relative minor, and that which is three in a minor key is one in its relative major.

What interval is produced by one and two of the minor scale? Two and three? Three and four? Four and five? Five and six? Six and seven? Seven and eight? How many keys are indicated by each signature in music? (*Ans.* Two.) *What are their names?* (*Ans.* Major and minor.) Give me the names of the keys as I give you the names of the signatures. *Natural?* (C major and A minor.) *One sharp?* (G major and E minor.) And so on through all.

CHAPTER XXXIV.

It will be well to direct the class to sing loud, soft, increasing or diminishing according to the requirements of the words; and it may aid them to do this, to practice the more unusual dynamic effects which may be done, as follows:

All sing to the pitch G, syllable *la*, a half note *pianissimo*. I write its abbreviation. Now *piano*; now *mezzo*; now *forte*; now *fortissimo*. I write the abbreviation of each, and the result is thus: *pp*   *p*   *m*   *f*   *ff*

Now I will pass my stick gradually from *pianissimo* to *fortissimo*. Take a good breath, and let your voices increase gradually as my stick goes. This gradual increasing is called in music CRESCENDO (pronounced *creshendo*), usually abbreviated in writing to *cres.*

Now all sing as I draw my stick gradually from *fortissimo* to *pianissimo*. This is called DIMINUENDO. Abbreviation, *dim.*

Now sing while I move my stick from *pianissimo* to *fortissimo* and back again, making both a *crescendo* and *diminuendo* in one breath. This is called a SWELL, and is sometimes indicated by the following character: ———————

Now be ready, for I shall go quickly. The teacher then moves his stick quickly from *pianissimo* through. When they have produced the effect well, he says, this is called a PRESSURE TONE, and is marked thus: <

Now the same the other way. This is one of the most important effects in dynamics. It is sometimes called the EXPLOSIVE TONE, and marked thus: > but is oftener called the FORZANDO, and indicated by   *fz* or *sfz*

Now sing the scale of C major, with syllable *la*, *crescendo* ascending, *diminuendo* descending.

Now again, giving each tone *forzando*.

In practicing these lessons in two parts, it is strongly recommended to divide the class equally, and let each section sing each part in turn. After a while it may be best to select those voices that are especially adapted to singing second, and let them always take that part. It is, however, desirable that all should be able to sing second when circumstances may require it; and this subject has not been introduced in this course until now, that the pupils may all be sufficiently independent to do this.

Question, before singing, with regard to key, kind of time, expression of words, major and minor, modulation and the proper use of the voice. Not, perhaps, all at each piece, but some at one and some at another—that the technical terms with regard to all these matters may be kept in mind.

No. 168.

1. Soft - ly   the shades of   even - ing come, Still - ing   the   gay world's
2. Gen - tly   the stars gleam   in   the   west, Zeph - yrs   have lulled   the

bus - y   hum.   So while   we   sing   our   last part - ing   lay,
birds to   rest.   Flash - ing   and   cool   the   brook - let   at   play,

Ritard. e dim.

Slow - ly   the   day - light fades   a - way, Fades a - way, fades a - way.
Mur - murs be - low, then glides   a - way, Glides a - way, glides a - way.

Ritard. means, to sing a little slower.

No. 169.

1. Night's shades no long - er   rest   on the   land, Bright - ly o'er   all doth
2. What scene so   love - ly, what scene so   fair,   As hill   and   vale   in

morn - ing ex - pand; Hail we   its   glo - ries   with heart   and with
morn's gold - en   air? Wake   to   their beau - ties,   a - wake heart and

voice: Come,   join   in   the   cho - rus,   re - joice,   O,   re - joice.
voice: Come,   join   in   the   cho - rus,   re - joice,   O,   re - joice.

No. 170. ALLEGRETTO.

1. Gai - ly the bright wings are flash - ing, Out in the mid-sum-mer
2. Wreaths of rare beau-ty we're twin - ing, Soon they will grace the sweet

air,   O - ver the flow - ers so ra - diant
bowers; Oh, in the gar - den so fra - grant,

Of the sweet gar-den so fair: Thou-sands of bright wings are
Swift - ly fly mo-ments and hours; While the bright wreaths we are

flash - ing, Out in the gar - den so fair.
twin - ing, Swift - ly fly mo - ments and hours.

No. 171.

1. On - ly be - gin - ing the jour - ney, Ma - ny a mile to go;
2. Talk-ing the odd - est lan - guage Ev - er be - fore was heard;
3. Fa-ther of all, O, guide them Pat - ter - ing lit - tle feet,

Lit - tle feet, see how they pat - ter, Wan - der - ing to and fro:
Moth-er (you will hard - ly think so) Un - der-stands ev - 'ry word:
While they are tread-ing the hill-road, Brav-ing the dust and heat!

Try - ing a - gain so brave - ly, Laugh-ing in ba - by glee;
Tot - ter - ing now and fall - ing, Eyes that are going to cry;
Aid them when they grow wea - ry, Keep them in path-ways blest;

Hid - ing its face by its moth - er, Proud as a child can be.
Kiss - es and plen - ty of love-words, Will-ing a - gain to try.
And when the jour - ney is end - ed, Sav-ior, O, give them rest.

No. 172.

1. Where sweet - est flow - ers grow, O list! list! list! And
2. Thy pres - ence here we greet, O stay! stay! stay! Thou

zeph-yrs mur-mur low; O list! list! list! I hear her step so
queen of flow-ers sweet, O stay! stay! stay! And wear the crown of

light and free; And, Oh, what peace and joy she brings to me.
sum - mer fair, Bright Flo - ra, with thy smiles and sun - ny hair.

No. 173.

1. Look a - way to the fields of the har - vest, See the
2. 'Tis the song of a true heart so hap - py, As he

reap - er a - mid the grain, How it rus - tles and trem-bles be-
gath - ers the shin - ing store, And he thinks of the soft hour of

fore him, Like the rain rip - ples on the main; And
twi - light When the la - bor of day is o'er; And

list!   he   sings,   As   he   sweeps o'er   the   gold - en   plain.
see!   he' smiles,   As   his   eye seeks   the   cot - tage   door.

No. 174.

1. Rain-drops are   fall - ing,   they   pat - ter   on   the   au-tumn leaves;
2. Yet 'tis not drear - y   with - in   our   qui - et   hap - py home,

Low winds are   sigh - ing   a - mid   the   bare and leaf - less trees:
While bright and cheer - y   a - round   our hearth the even-ings come;

Gone are   all   the sweet flow'rs, and   the   sum-mer's bright hours
Though we mourn the sweet flow'rs, au - tumn fruits are now ours;

Mourn - ful - ly   sing   in   the   chill   and des - o - lat - ed bowers.
So   we   will   not   heed   the storm-king's dark and win-t'ry powers.

No. 175.

1. O, how   sweet are   the   ech - oes   at   even - ing, When the
2. And the   riv - er   be - low   gen - tly   moan - ing, Hath a

vil - lage a-round us   is   still,   Of   the shep-herd boy's pipe soft-ly
charm in the tone of its   song,   As   all   dim in the shade of the

peal - ing, As he watch - es his flock on the hill:
gleam - ing, Its clear wa - ters flow light - ly a - long:

'Tis the song of con - tent - ment and bless - ing, And it
How the moon in her splen - dor on ris - ing, Loves to

spreads far a - way o'er the dale; To the wea - ry it comes with ca-
mir - ror her face in the deep; While the breez - es with soft ca-dence

ress - ing, To the sad with a sil - ver - y veil.
sigh - ing, Lulls the for - est to shad - ow - y sleep.

No. 176.

1. Stud - y hard, stud - y hard, In the school-room, day by day; Stud - y
2. Stud - y hard, stud - y hard, Youth is short and life is long; Stud - y
3. Stud - y hard, stud - y hard, If you learn your les-sons well; Stud - y
4. Stud - y hard, stud - y hard, Pass no les - son i - dly by; Stud - y

Stud - y hard...................

hard, stud - y hard, Put a - side your i - dle play,   Stud - y hard,
hard, stud - y hard, School-days swift-ly glide a-long,   Stud - y hard,
hard, stud - y hard, Time a - lone their use will tell,   Stud - y hard,
hard, stud - y hard, You can learn if you will try,   Stud - y hard,

stud - y hard...................   stud - y hard...............

stud - y hard,   stud - y hard, stud - y hard.

It is quite common, especially in songs for young people, to put two staves together, with two parts on each staff, as in the following example, making four parts that may be sung at the same time. It will be an excellent plan to sing the four parts of this tune, first with syllables, and then with the words set; although it is expected, that in the music of this book generally there will be but one or two parts sung (those on the upper staves), and the music is arranged to sound well in this way. It will, however, be an advantage to have an instrument, or voices, give all the parts.

The character connecting the two staves together is called a BRACE.

No. 177.

Now four parts to - geth - er, We'll burst in - to a song,

The meas - ure gen - tly flow - ing, The pleas - ant tones pro - long;

Then loud - er, and loud - er, Our mu - sic fills the air,

And ech - oes, and ech - oes, O'er hill and val - ley fair.

CONCERT, SCHOOL AND HOME.

If I were a Bird.

MODERATO.

1. [1]Were I   a   bird, I would [2]soar on high, [3]And clap my wings as   I
2. [4]I'd wheel and float thro' the bright blue air, [5]Then drop be-low   to   the
3. [6]I'd   fly   a - way to a   shel-ter'd nook, [7]And build my nest by   the
4. [8]I'd swing and rock on my down - y nest, [9]And smooth my feath-ers for
5. [6]In morn-ing's light I would swift-ly speed [10]Where bus-y hands sow the
6. [4]O'er broad green fields I would sing and roam, [6]Then hie a - way to   my

cleaved the   sky, [3]And   clap   my wings as   I   cleaved the   sky.
mead - ows   fair, [5]Then   drop   be - low   to   the   mead - ows fair.
mur-m'ring brook, [7]And build   my   nest by   the   mur-m'ring brook.
even - ing's rest, [9]And smooth my   feath - ers   for   even - ing's rest.
pre - cious seed, [10]Where bus - y   hands sow   the   pre - cious seed.
own sweet [1]home, [6]Then   hie   a - way   to   my   own sweet [1]home.

1 Arms folded
2 Raise both arms, pointing upward.
3 Arms fall heavily.
4 Describe circles above the head.
5 Imitate bird plunging down.

6 Wave arms as if flying.
7 Tapping on seat with fingers.
8 Swing the arms.
9 Pass hands from head downward.
10 Imitate sowing grain.

6
79

Vacation Over.—Exercise Song.

ALLEGRETTO.

1. Should old com-pan-ions be for - got, And bro't to mind no more?
2. Should faith-ful teach-ers, true and tried, Be bro't to mind no more?
3. Then, friends, com-pan-ions, hap-py band, We'll pledge our hearts once more,

Should old com-pan-ions be for - got, And the bright days gone be-fore?
They've stood with pa-tience by our side, In the bright days gone be-fore;
We'll walk to - geth - er hand in hand, In the bright days yet be-fore;

O, no, O, no, we'll ne'er for-get, We'll greet each school-mate dear;
O, no, O, no, we'll ne'er for-get, We'll greet our teach - ers dear;
O, no, O, no, we'll ne'er for-get, Com - pan-ions, school-mates dear;

We'll give a [1]nod of kind-ness yet, And a heart - y wel-come here.
We'll give a [2]nod of kind-ness yet, And a heart - y wel-come here.
We'll give a [1]nod of kind-ness yet, And a heart - y wel-come here.

1 Graceful bow to schoolmates.   2 Graceful bow to teachers.

FIRST DIVISION.   ALLEGRETTO.

1. Did you ev - er see the farm - er sow, In the spring-time of the year?
2. Did you ev - er see the mow - er mow, When the grass was high and tall?
3. Did you ev - er see the reap - er reap, In the au - tumn of the year?
4. Did you ev - er see the thresh-er thresh, When the wheat was gath-er'd in?

When all the fields were get - ting green, And the skies were blue and clear?
He swings his scythe with meas-ur'd beat, And the slen - der grass - es fall.
When all the fields were get - ting brown, And the sky was blue and clear?
And the corn was borne from the field and piled In the hap - py farm - er's bin?

SECOND DIVISION.

This is the way that the farm - er sows, In the spring-time of the year;
This is the way that the farm - er mows, When the grass is high and tall;
This is the way that the reap - er reaps, In the au - tumn of the year;
This is the way that the thresh-ers thresh, When the wheat is gath-er'd in;

When all the fields are grow - ing green, And the skies are blue and clear.
He swings his scythe with meas - ur'd beat, And the slen - der grass - es fall.
When all the fields are get - ting brown, And the skies are blue and clear.
And the corn is borne from the field, and piled In the hap - py farm - er's bin.

Let the motions commence at the second division, and keep time with the music.

The Old School-House.—Exercise Song.

MODERATO.

1. If we stamp our feet to keep us warm, The teach-er thinks we're
2. Un-cle Sam is rich, we all know that; I wish he'd try to
3. There is wood e-nough to make the boards, And saws e-nough to

naught-y; It's hard to keep your-self per-fect-ly calm, With
please us: It's hard to live in a ver-y old hut, While
saw it; If Un-cle Sam, or if some-bod-y else, Would

CHORUS.

weath-er down to for-ty. Then [1]stamp, [1]stamp, [1]stamp, [1]stamp! We will
Un-cle 's rich as Crœ-sus. Then, &c.
find the team to draw it. Then, &c.

make the old house [2]ring; [3]There's no use [3]freez-ing your-

1 Stamp with feet, not too loud. | 2 Strike hands together. | 3 Rubbing and swinging the hands.

self 'to death In the poor old shell of a ²thing.

The Launch.—Exercise Song.

Moderato.

1. ¹Our beau - ti - ful ship is launch'd to - day; ²Glo - rious day!
2. ¹Our beau - ti - ful ship is launch'd to - day; ⁴Clear the way!
3. ¹Our beau - ti - ful ship is launch'd to - day; ⁵Down she goes!

²glo - rious day! ³We'll strike the blow that sets her free;
⁴clear the way! ³In un - ion, then, all hands once ³more,
⁵down she goes! ⁴She sweeps the blue waves' spark - ling spray;

²Glo-rious day! ²glo-rious day!
⁴Clear the way! ⁴clear the way!
⁵Down she goes! ⁵down she goes!

4. ¹Our beautiful ship is launch'd to-day,
   ⁶Roll the drum! ⁶roll the drum!
   ²We'll wave the glorious banner high,
   ⁶Roll the drum! ⁶roll the drum!

5. ¹Our beautiful ship is launch'd to-day,
   ⁷There she floats! ⁷there she floats!
   ²Hurrah for noble ship and crew!
   ⁷There she floats! ⁷there she floats!

1 Arms folded. •
2 Describe circles above head.
3 Strike hands together.
4 Hands moved as in swimming.
5 Hands plunged downward.
6 Beat time.
7 Extend arms with waving motion or undulations.

1. Come, and stand be - side me, chil-dren, Let me talk a - while with you.
2. Can you tell me which way, chil-dren, It is north, and which way south?
3. Can you tell me which way, chil-dren, It is east, and which way west?

We will come and stand be - side you, We will talk a - while with you.
We can tell you that, dear teach-er, *That* is north, and *that* is south.
We can tell you that, dear teach-er, *That* is east, and *that* is west.

Teacher.   4. Can you tell me which way, children,
                   Europe is from where we stand?
Children.   We can tell you that, dear teacher,
                   Europe's *east* from where we stand.

Teacher.   5. Can you tell me which way, children,
                   Europe is from Africa?
Children.   We can tell you that, dear teacher,
                   Europe's *north* of Africa.

Teacher.   6. Can you tell me which way, children,
                   Asia's from America?
Children.   We can tell you that, dear teacher,
                   Asia's *east* from 'Merica.

Teacher.   7. You have answered well, dear children,
                   You have answered very well.
Children.   We are glad that we can answer
                   Questions that you ask, so well.

In answer to the first two lines, sung by the teacher, the pupils should take their place on the floor. When answering the questions relative to the "*cardinal points*," they will point according to the answers of the questions asked. They will also point in the direction of Europe, when answering that it is east of America. North, when answering, Europe is north of Africa. When the last verse is sung, they will all bow to the teacher, and take their seats in order. If the teacher does not choose to sing, a section or single voice among the pupils may be appointed to ask the questions.

What the Birds are Saying.—Exercise Song.

FIRST DIVISION.

1. Hear the quail in yon - der glen, He is call - ing to his
2. Hear the owl from yon - der tree, Hid a - mong the leaves so
3. Seek-ing for his morn - ing food, Hear the crow in yon - der
4. When the even - ing comes a - gain, And the earth in night is

mate; You can hear him in the morn - ing, Hear him
green; Can you tell me what he's say - ing, In his
field; He must feed the lit - tle nest - lings, In the
hid; Then a - long the roads and mead - ows, You will

SECOND DIVISION.

ear - ly, hear him late: Whu, whu, whuit; whu, whu, whuit;
leaf - y house un - seen: Whoo, whoo, who-o-o! Whoo, whoo, who-o-o!
nest so well con-cealed: Caw! caw! caw! Caw! caw! caw!
hear the ka - ty - did: Ka - ty, katy-did! Ka - ty, katy-did!

That is what the quail is say-ing, As he whis-tles to his mate.
That is what the owl is say-ing, In his leaf - y house un - seen.
That is what the crow is say-ing, As he seeks his nest-lings' food.
All a - long the roads and mead-ows, Thus the ka - ty - dids will sing.

Children can easily imitate the quail, but it is very difficult to render his whistle in words.

We are standing Face to Face.—EXERCISE SONG.

1. We are stand-ing face to face, Each one in his pro - per place;
2. Let us whirl a - bout once more, Take of steps, one, two, three, four,
3. Put one hand be - hind you, so, One up - on your breast, you know;
4. Let us all keep time once more, With our right foot on the floor;
5. Wave your right hand up and down, Keep-ing time with words and sound;

Let us step, one, two, three, four, Then we'll all shake hands once more.
'Till we reach our right - ful place, Then we'll turn round face to face.
Change them quick-ly left and right, This will be a pleas - ant sight.
Now our left one we will try, While we hold our hands on high.
Let us to our teach - er bow, For our stud - ies call us now.

CHORUS.

O, 'tis pleas-ant to be here, In our health ful ex - er - cise;

Let us in it per - se - vere, 'Till we make our work pre-cise.

The children should stand nine steps apart, and at the words "*one, two,*" &c., step toward each other, and shake hands. In the chorus, let them keep time with their hands. In third verse, let them put one hand behind them, the other on their breast. Then let them bring their left hand around to their breast, and carry their right one behind them, *both at the same time.*

Twice one are two, That is ver-y true; Twice two are four,
D. C. There, that will do; Now we've sung all thro', Well was it done,

That's a cou-ple more; Twice three are six, On this our min ds we'll
Soon pre-pare for fun; When this we know, We will still far-ther

FINE.

fix; Twice four are eight, We will not be late. Twice five are ten,
go, Hop-ing we may All know more some day.

We'll be lit-tle men; Twice six are twelve, For learn-ing we must

delve; Twice seven are four-teen, Bad we'll be no more seen; Twice eight are

six-teen, Glass with put-ty sticks in; Twice nine are eight-een,

Let each keep his slate clean; Twice ten are twen-ty, We will all learn

plen-ty; Twice 'leven are twen-ty-two, We'll at-tend to what we do;

Twice twelve are twen-ty-four, That's the last, there are no more.

Multiplication Song.—Concluded.

Five times five are twen - ty - five, And five times six are thir - ty, And

five times seven are thir - ty - five, And five times eight are for - ty;

Five times nine are for - ty - five, Five times ten are fif - ty,

D. C.

Five times 'leven are fif - ty - five, Five times twelve are six - ty.

Steady, Boys!—Exercise Song.

MODERATO.

1. ¹Stead - y, boys! stead - y, boys! mind your team! ²There's
2. ¹Stead - y, boys! stead - y, boys! En - gi - neer! ²The
3. ¹Stead - y, boys! stead - y, boys! don't you hear! ⁵The

some-thing the mat - ter, the mat - ter, the mat - ter! ³The
cars are in dread - ful com - mo - tion, com - mo - tion! ²They
steam - er is puff - ing, and reel - ing and rock - ing! ³The

joints are all loose, and the box - es they scream! ²The
rat - tle, and clat - ter, and rum - ble and roar! ³The
boil - ers are hiss - ing and scream - ing, O. dear! ²The

bolts are a - clat - ter, a - clat - ter, a - clat - ter: ⁶It's an
world is in mo - tion, com - mo - tion, com - mo - tion: ⁶It's an
thump - ing, and groan - ing and strain - ing is shock - ing: ⁶It's an

aw - ful rough road, or some-thing's to pay; ⁴The driv - er is
aw - ful rough road, or some-thing's to pay; ⁴The driv - er is
aw - ful rough sea, or some-thing's to pay; ⁴The cap - tain is

drunk, ¹And the hors - es are run - ning a - way!
drunk, ¹And the en - gines are run - ning a - way!
drunk, ¹And the steam - boat is run - ning a - way!

1 Hands held as if driving horses.
2 Rattling feet or hands.
3 Twirl hands around each other.

4 This line recited in a whisper.
5 Swaying body to and fro.
6 Extend the hands as cautious persons would

Drummer Boy. (Exercise Song.)

G. F. R.

MARCH MOVEMENT.

I. 1Drum-mer boy, drum-mer boy, where are you speed-ing, 2Roll-ing so
2. 1Col - or boy, col - or boy, where are you hie - ing, 3Wav-ing your
3. 1Sol - dier boy, sol - dier boy, where are you go - ing, 4Bear-ing, so

gai - ly your bold rat - a - plan? 1I go where my coun-try my
ban - ner of red, white and blue? 1I go where the flag of the
proud - ly your knap-sack and gun? 1I go where my coun-try my

ser - vice is need - ing, 2Roll-ing, so gai - ly my bold rat - a - plan.
free should be fly - ing, 3Wav-ing my ban - ner of red, white and blue.
du - ty is show - ing, 4Bear-ing so proud-ly my knap-sack and gun.

4. 1When will you come again, soldier-boys, playing,
2Drumming, and 3waving, and 4bearing the gun?
1Not while our country shall bid us be staying,
2Drumming, and 3waving, and 4bearing the gun.

5. 2Rat-a-plan-plan, not a "white feather" showing,
3Follow the glorious red, white and blue;
1Sing us a song as we gaily are going,
Sing us a song, then, adieu, boys, adieu!

1 Hands folded.
2 Keep time to the music with the ends of the fingers on the desk.
3 Wave the right hand, or little flags in the right hand.
4 Lay the hands upon the shoulders.

Charlie wants a Piece of Bread. (EXERCISE SONG.)

ALLEGRETTO.   B. R. II.

[Musical notation]

1. ¹Char - lie wants a piece of bread, ²Bes - sie says there is none;
2 ⁴Round the mill goes, in the wind; If of flour there is none,

³Knead some dough, then, Bes - sie, knead, But of flour there is none.
Grind some grain, good mil - ler, grind, ²But of wheat there is none.

3. ⁵Sow some grain, good farmer, sow,
 If of wheat there is none;
 ⁶Come, soft showers, and make it grow,
 ²For of bread there is none.

4. ⁷Thresh it on the threshing floor,
 ²For of bread there is none;
 ⁴Grind it, miller, o'er and o'er,
 ²Till of bread there is some.

5. ⁸Knead it quick, good Bessie, knead,
 ²Now of flour there is some;
 ¹Charlie, here's your piece of bread—
 ²Are n't you glad there is some?

6. ⁵Sow, and ⁷thresh, and ⁴grind, and ³knead,
 ²When of bread there is none;
 ⁶What a deal of work, indeed.
 ²Just for bread there is done.

1 Both hands stretched out.
2 Fold hands.
8 Move hands as in kneading bread.
4 Move right hand to imitate a wind mill.

5 Move right hand as in sowing seed.
6 Move fingers on the desk to imitate rain sounds
7 Both arms up and down as in threshing.
9 Both hands raised perpendicularly.

ALLEGRETTO

1. ¹Rap! ¹rap! ¹rap! ¹rap! How the shing - les ²clap
2. ¹Nail, ¹boys, ¹nail! ¹nail, Nev - er mind the ²gale,
3. ⁶Rest, now rest, rest, What a co - sy nest!

³Here a beam and ⁴there a tim - ber, ⁵Then a ⁵board so ⁵long and ⁵lim-ber.
³Sun - ny days. or win - dy ⁴weather ⁵Cheerful ⁵la - bor ⁵all to⁵geth - er.
³All well done from floor to ga - ble, ⁴Mim-ic shelf and kitch-en ta - ble;

How the laths shall ²snap, ²snap, How the ham - mer's ¹rap!
Soon our house we'll ²hail, ²hail, Brisk - ly ¹nail, ¹boys, ¹nail!
⁶Now sit down and rest, rest, All have done your best.

1 Rap with ends of fingers of both hands on the desks.
2 Bring the hands together with one clap.
3 Wave right hand to the right and leave it there.

4 Wave left hand to the left and leave it there.
5 Move both hands up and down, waving time to the music.
6 Fold hands.

Now Work is Done.—ROUND.

Now work is done, and we'll go home, O come a - long boys come.

1. There's a bright fire in the forge. And the iron is heat-ing fast;
2. Now the fur-nace roars a-loud, Throw-ing light through all the shop;
3. Put it in the fire a-gain, 'Tis not whol-ly shaped as yet;
4. Rake the ash-es o'er the fire, Work is done, the shoe is made;

By his an-vil stands the smith, While the bel-lows give the blast.
Pull the iron out, strike it fast, 'Till it's cold you must not stop.
Blow by blow, with pa-tient work, What a horse-shoe we shall get!
Rest a-while, the toil is hard, Yet it is a mer-ry trade.

CHORUS.

Bang! bang! bang! bang! Oh how hard the ham-mers strike!

Bang! bang! bang! bang! That's the tune we like.

NOTE.—The class is separated into two divisions. During the chorus these divisions mark the time as follows:—At the first "bang" the first division hit the desk with their closed fists, at the second "bang" the second division do the same; at the third, the first ag in; at the fourth, the second, and so on alternating to the end of the chorus.

Jolly Little Clacker.—Exercise Song.

G. F. R.

[Wherever the words "click" and "clack" occur, the fingers may be snapped, or the hands struck together; or, better still, when convenient the "bones" may be used. At the word "click," the sound should be softer than at "clack."]

Moderato.

1. Spring-time brings the Rob-in and the Blue Bird home: The
2. Through the nos-y mar-ket, down the long pa-rade, Up-
3. Blue Bird and the swal-low from the sweet South rove, The
4. Move your nim-ble fin-gers in the brisk, quick way; Some

hap-py lit-tle Swal-low knows his hour to come; But
on the crowd-ed side-walk,'neath the com-mon's shade, His
Rob-in leaves his quar-ters, in the deep pine grove; I
peo-ple could not do it, if they tried all day! This

not a bird is tru-er to his time of com-ing back Than the
tramp-ing feet for mu-sic in their march-ing can-not lack, While his
know from whence they start-ed on the hap-py home-ward track; But where
morn the first of clack-ers, but a hun-dred know the knack, And to-

p

jol-ly lit-tle clack-er, with his clack, clack, clack! Click, click, click,
nim-ble lit-tle fin-gers play the clack, clack, clack! Click, &c.
all the win-ter sleep-ing, stays the clack, clack, clack? Click, &c.
night you'll hear them an-swer with a clack, clack, clack! Click, &c.

clack, clack, clack! Jol - ly lit - tle clack-er, with your clack, clack, clack!

Whip-poor-will.   B. R. H.

1. O'er fra - grant sum - mer fields, new mown, When eve comes down and
2. As clos - er fold the shades of night, And bright - er shine the
3. At mid - night, when the moon, se - rene, With glo - ry gilds the
4. He sings up - on the ma - ple high, Or in the fra - grant
5. In oth - er lands the Night - in - gales Sing, all night long, in

day is flown, I hear up - on the dis - tant hill, Whip-poor-will,
stars of light, Sounds, near-er, by the tink - ling rill, Whip-poor-will,
si - lent scene, Bursts, start-ling, o'er my dwell - ing still, Whip-poor-will,
li - lacs nigh; A - far or on my win - dow sill, Whip-poor-will,
moon - lit vales; But thy sad strains our nights shall fill. Whip-poor-will,

Whip-poor-will, whip-poor-will, whip-poor-will, whip-poor-will, whip-poor-will!

Was it right?

B. R. H.

MODERATO.

1. If the boys and girls will list-en,
2. All their books so new and pret-ty,
3. Then a-long the street came, sing-ing,

I will tell them in my song, Of a
Lay up-on the dust-y ground; They were
Such a mer-ry lit-tle lad; But his

sad thing that I no-ticed, As to school I came a-long;
torn, and soiled and tum-bled, As their own-ers pushed a-round,
song soon ceased its ring-ing, And his hap-py face was sad,

'Twas a fight! 'twas a fight! 'twas a fight! 'Twas be-
In such plight, in such plight, in such plight; That they
At the sight, at the sight, at the sight; And he

tween two lit - tle chil - dren, Who had fall - en out in play;
nev - er will be de - cent To be used in school a - gain;
part - ed them so gen - tly, And he begged them so, to cease,

And, a - las! they beat each oth - er In a
But the boys had both for - got - ten All a-
That they twined their arms to - geth - er, And all

rude and an - gry way! Was it right? was it right? was it right?
bout their les-sons then. Was it right? was it right? was it right?
went to school in peace. That was right! that was right! that was right!

Be Kind and True.—Round.

Be kind and true In all that you may do, Keep this in view.

7

Jolly Little Clacker.—Exercise Song. G. F. R.

[Wherever the words "click" and "clack" occur, the fingers may be snapped, or the hands struck together; or, better still, when convenient the "bones" may be used. At the word "click," the sound should be softer than at "clack."]

MODERATO.

1. Spring-time brings the Rob - in and the Blue Bird home: The
2. Through the nois - y mar - ket, down the long pa - rade, Up-
3. Blue Bird and the swal - low from the sweet South rove, The
4. Move your nim - ble fin - gers in the brisk, quick way; Some

hap - py lit - tle Swal-low knows his hour to come; But
on the crowd - ed side-walk, 'neath the com-mon's shade, His
Rob - in leaves his quar - ters, in the deep pine grove; I
peo - ple could not do it, if they tried all day! This

not a bird is tru - er to his time of com-ing back Than the
tramp-ing feet for mu - sic in their march-ing can-not lack, While his
know from whence they start-ed on the hap-py home-ward track; But where
morn the first of clack-ers, but a hun-dred know the knack, And to-

jol - ly lit - tle clack-er, with his clack, clack, clack! Click, click, click,
nim - ble lit - tle fin-gers play the clack, clack, clack! Click, &c.
all the win-ter sleep-ing, stays the clack, clack, clack? Click, &c.
night you'll hear them an-swer with a clack, clack, clack! Click, &c.

clack, clack, clack! Jol - ly lit - tle clack-er, with your clack, clack, clack!

Whip-poor-will.

B. R. H.

1. O'er fra - grant sum - mer fields, new mown, When eve comes down and
2. As clos - er fold the shades of night, And bright - er shine the
3. At mid - night, when the moon, se - rene, With glo - ry gilds the
4. He sings up - on the ma - ple high, Or in the fra - grant
5. In oth - er lands the Night - in - gales Sing, all night long, in

day is flown, I hear up - on the dis - tant hill, Whip-poor-will,
stars of light, Sounds, near - er, by the tink - ling rill, Whip-poor-will,
si - lent scene, Bursts, start - ling, o'er my dwell - ing still, Whip-poor-will,
li - lacs nigh; A - far or on my win - dow sill, Whip-poor-will,
moon - lit vales; But thy sad strains our nights shall fill. Whip-poor-will,

Whip-poor-will, whip-poor-will, whip-poor-will, whip-poor-will, whip-poor-will!

The Cars are Coming.—Exercise Song. W. J. R.

ALLEGRETTO.

1. It is time, time, time that the peo - ple were wide a-
2. Come, a - rouse, rouse, rouse ye, and ral - ly with might and
3. All ye youth, youth, youth of the land, hear the call once

wake; Our lives and our for - tunes are all at stake; A-
main, To scat - ter the for - ces of Rum a - gain; Our
more, The train is ap-proach-ing, the night is o'er; For

rouse, or you'll find your - selves late in the day, The
cause is ad - vanc - ing, hur - rah for the fray, The
Tem - per - ance Sta - tion our bag - gage we'll check, Re-

CHORUS.

cars are on time, and they nev - er de - lay. The cars are com-ing,
cars are on time, and they nev - er de - lay. The cars, &c.
solve to be so - ber and keep on the track. The cars, &c.

com-ing,   com-ing, The wheels are roll-ing,   roll-ing,   roll-ing, Stand

out of the way there, clear the track, This en-gine goes for-ward, but

nev - er goes back; [1]The cars are com-ing,   com-ing,   com-ing, [1]The

wheels are roll - ing, roll - ing, roll - ing, [2]Hur-rah for Tem-p'rance

1 Keeping time with the hands.   2 Swinging hats or handkerchiefs.

The Happy Band.—Exercise Song.

G. F. R.

MODERATO.

1. [1] A hap - py band in free-dom's land, [2] We do just as we like to;
2. [1] A hap - py band in free-dom's land, [2] We do just as we like to:
3. [1] A hap - py band in free-dom's land, [3] We do just as we like to;
4. [1] A hap - py band in free-dom's land, [2] We do just as we like to;

[3] Provided we do what's right, and that is what we calculate to do [11] always. We

[3] Provided we do just what our teacher wishes us to do, and are not [11] [11] eye-
servants.
We

[8] We now propose to take a drink of freedom's pure air.
We

[8] We liked the other drink of freedom's pure air so well, that we now
take another.
'Tis

[4] swing our arms and [5] clap our hands, And [6] bind our brows with gold-en bands,

[14] fling our un-chain'd arms on high, Like [14] free-dom's ban-ners in the sky,

[9] fill our lungs with free-dom's air, And [10] gaze o'er free-dom's land so fair,

[12] like the nec - tar of the gods, It [13] makes us strong for ev - 'ry odds,

And do just as we [7] like to.
And do just as we [7] like to.
And do just as we [7] like to.
To do just as we like [11] to.

1 Hands folded.——2 Arms looped out, with hands resting on thigh.——3 Recite in concert in speaking voice.——4 Swing arms.——5 Clap hands.——6 Right arm raise above head, hand bent downward and passed around head.—— 7 Strike softly on head or shoulder of nearest schoolmate (not intended for naughty boys).—— 8 First 3, then fold arms behind, then fill the lungs by drawing in slowly until all give out. ——9 Hands placed on lungs.——10 Sweep arms around to touch behind.——11 Bring right hand to forehead, and sweep it outward and downward, bowing the head at the same time.——12 Hands clasped before.——13 Arms flung outward, with hands clenched, expressing strength.——14 Both hands describe circles above the head.

1. At dew - y dawn, in mist - y morn, When o'er the wood-lands,
2. And when she goes, where, sing - ing, flows The brook's blue wa - ter
3. But, ah! one day, I blush to say, When she was wild and
4. But what a shame to bear such name, To be so rude and

hill - y, Her lit - tle feet fly swift and fleet, We
chill - y, And plash - es thro' the wave - let blue, We
wil - ly. And strove at bay, to - have her way, We
sil - ly, She'll try, I'm sure, to be so pure, We'll

call her Mead - ow - Lil - y, Oh, yes, Oh,
call her Wa - ter - Lil - y, Oh, yes, Oh,
called her Ti - ger - Lil - y, Oh, yes, Oh,
call her sweet Day Lil - y, Oh, yes, Oh,

yes, yes,

yes, We call her Mead - ow - Lil - y.
yes, We call her Wa - ter - Lil - y.
yes, We called her Ti - ger - Lil - y.
yes, We'll call her sweet Day - Lil - y.

yes, yes,

O, we have Studied Hard now. u. f. r.

MODERATO

1. O we have stud ied hard now, For twen-ty weeks or more, It
2. "All work-ing and no play - ing, Makes Jack a stu - pid boy," It
3. I love the dear old school-room, I love the teach-ers more; But

seems as though *we'd like a rec - re - a - tion; My
seems to me, *this is a truth - ful say - ing; 'Tis
then a rest, * would give us bet - ter na - ture, We'll

head is grow-ing wea - ry, My pulse is get - ting slower; O
true to my ex - pe-rience, And grow-ing so still more; I
all come back and stud - y, When days of rest are o'er, And

CHORUS
ALLEGRETTO

yes we'd like *a re - al good va - ca - tion. Wait a lit - tle
wish 'twere done, *and we were out a play - ing. Wait &c.
pledge our word*of hon - or for the fu - ture. Wait &c.

long - er boys, Wait a lit - tle long - er; Don't give up the

ship to - day, But wait a lit - tle long - er;

La - bor makes the mo-ments fly, La - bor wins the glo - ry;

We shall con-quer by - and - bye And sing an - oth - er sto - ry.

*At this rest with the pause over it, an amusing effect may be produced by allowing the class to yawn or gape or sigh, as if weary. Take time enough to do it naturally and be careful to come in well together afterwards.

The young Recruits.—Exercise Song.

G. F. R.

MAESTOSO

1. ¹This day's a ²glo-rious day, my ²boys! A ⁷glo rious ⁶day for
2. Now load your guns with am-mu-nition, And fill them up with
3. Now please take ⁹aim right at the mark; ¹⁰No low-er now nor
4. ¹You dull boy there! hold up your head! ¹⁰Let all the rest take

³free-dom! ²The ⁴or : der's come to ⁴march, my boys, ²And
pow-der; And ⁸all say ⁷··bang!" as ⁸loud's you ³can, To
high-er! And ⁸shoot your guns off when I ³speak, Just
warn-ing; Now ¹¹shoul-der arms, and ⁸for-ward, ³march! The

I'm the man to lead em; ⁶Left and ⁴Right, ⁶Left and ⁴Right, ⁷At-
make the guns go loud-er; ⁶Left and ⁴Right, ⁶Left and ⁴Right, ⁷At-
⁸when the word goes, ⁷"fire!" ⁶Left and ⁴Right, ⁶Left and ⁴Right, ⁷At-
²day of glo-ry's dawn-ing; ⁶Left and ⁴Right, ⁶Left and ⁴Right, ⁷At-

INTERLUDE. (may be whistled.)

ten - tion! ⁶for-ward! ³march!
ten - tion! ⁶for-ward! ³march!
ten - tion! ⁶for-ward! ³march!
ten - tion! ⁶for-ward! ³march!

1 Arms folded behind; head erect.
2 Describe circles above the head.
3 Bring arms down to side with a clap.
4 Right foot down.
6 Left foot down.

7 Bring hands together with a clap.
8 Fling arms outward, right and left.
9 Arms as if taking aim.
10 Raise right hand.
11 Hands on shoulders.

Kitty Dew-drop.

F. R.

MODERATO

1. To what shall we lik - en our Kit - ty, Our
2. Like dew she makes fair things seem fair - er, Like
3. Like dew-drops at noon and at e - ven, Our
4. And so, when her la - bors are end - ing, Life's

Kit - ty so young and so gay? She's just like the dew-drop, so
dew she makes bright things more bright ; Like dewdrops, with others a
Kit - ty must hast - en to bear Some-what of the fresh-ness of
la - bors of mer - cy and love, Like dew on the sun-beams as-

pret - ty, That glis - tens at dawn of the day.
shar - er In all of her sim - ple de - light.
Heav - en To souls that are droop - ing with care.
cend - ing, She'll shine in the gar - den a - bove.

By permission of H. Tolman & Co.

E. C. D.

1. The ground was all cov - er'd with
2. He had not been sing - ing that

snow one day, And two lit - tle sis - ters were
tune very long, Ere Em - i - ly heard him, so

bu - sy at play, When a snow bird was sit - ting close
loud was his song. "O sis - ter, look out of the

by on a tree; And mer - ri - ly sing - ing his
win - dow," said she, "Here's a dear lit - tle bird sing - ing

106

chick - a - de - de, chick - a - de - de, chick - a - de - de,

And mer - ri - ly sing - ing his chick - a - de - de.

3. Poor fellow! he walks in the snow and the sleet,
And has neither stockings nor shoes on his feet;
I pity him so! Oh how cold he must be!
And yet he keeps singing his chick-a-de-de.—Chick-a-de-de, &c.

4. If I were a barefooted snow-bird, I know
I would not stay out in the cold and the snow
I wonder what makes him so full of his glee:
He's all the time singing that chick-a-de-de.- Caick-a-de-de, &c.

5. O mother! do get him some stockings and snoes,
A frock, with a cloak and a hat, if he choose;
I wish he'd come into the parlor, and see
How warm we would make him, poor chick-a-de-de.–Chick-a-de-de,&c.

6. The bird had flown down for some pieces of bread,
And heard every word little Emily said;
"What a figure I'd make in that dress!" thought he
And he laughed as he warbled his chick-a-de-de.—Chick-a-de-de, &c.

7. "I am grateful," he said, "for the wish you express,
But I've no occasion for such a fine dress;
I had rather remain with my limbs all free,
Than to hobble about singing chick-a-de-de.—Chick-a-de-de, &c.

8. "There's One, my dear child, though I cannot tell who,
.Has clothed me already, and warm enough too:
Good morning! O who are so happy as we!"
And away he went, singing his chick-a-de-de.—Chick-a-de-de, &c.

Playing Bird.

G. F. R.

MODERATO.

1. "Let's all be birds," said Min - nie, When the morn - ing task was
done; "I'm tired of play - ing our oth - er plays, And
this is the pret-tiest one." "Yes," cried the chil - dren, glad - ly,
As they put their books a - way. "We haven't play'd this for-
ev - er so long, So we'll play it a - gain to - day.

[For the following verses it will be sometimes necessary to divide or join the notes of the tune a little differently from what they are for the first verse, in order to accommodate the accent and number of syllables; but it will not be difficult to arrange.]

2. "I'll be a thrush," said Minnie,
   "And sing you my sweetest song,
And have my nest where the lilies blow
   And the streamlet glides along."
"I," said her little sister,
   "Oh! I'll be a little wren,
And sing all day 'till the sun goes
   down,
   And the world grows dark again."

3. "I'll be a crow," said Willie,
   "And the farmers' corn I'll pull;
And that'll let some of the mischief
   out,
   For of mischief I am full."
"I'll be a great proud eagle,
   And my home shall be the sky,"
Said Johnny, "and I'll go sailing swift
   The clouds and the mountains by."

4. "I'll be an owl," said Henry,
   "And sit in an old oak tree,
And all the rest of the little birds
   Shall be so 'fraid of me."
"I'll be a lark," said Mary,
   "And sing at the break of day;"
"And I'll be a hawk," said Philip
   Lee,
   "And frighten the lark away."

5. "I'll be a *man*," said Georgy,
   And his little face grew bright;
"For a man knows more than all the
   birds;"
   And the little boy was right.
"If there's a man among us,"
   Said the pretty little wren,
"I think we'd all better fly away,
   For birds are afraid of men."

Vowel and Consonant Exercise.

B, a, ba; b, e, be; b, i, bi, ba, be, bi; b, o, bo, ba, be,

bi, bo; b, u, bu, ba, be, bi, bo, bu; A, e, i, o, u.

The above will be easily learned by the little ones, and afford them great amusement, as well as profit. After learning the tune, let them take the other consonants in their order, thus: D, a, da; d, e, de, &c. All the consonants in the alphabet may be used, except C, G, Q and X.

1. A - way! a - way! the track is white, The stars are shin - ing
2. A - way! a - way! our hearts are gay, And need not breathe by
3. A - way! a - way! a - cross the plain, We sweep as sea - birds

clear to-night, The win-ter winds are sleep-ing; The moon a-bove the
night or day, A sigh for sum-mer pleas-ure; The mer-ry bells ring
skim the main, Our puls - es gai - ly leap-ing; The stars are bright, the

stee - ple tall, A sil - ver cres - cent, o - ver all, Her
gai - ly out, Our lips keep time with song and shout, And
track is white, There's joy in ev - 'ry heart to - night, While

si - lent watch is keep - ing, Her si - lent watch is keep - ing.
laugh in hap - py meas - ure, And laugh in hap - py meas - ure.
win - ter winds are sleep - ing, While win - ter winds are sleep - ing.

Then jin - gle, jin - gle, jin - gle, jin - gle, Bells and hoofs are gay;

Clack! clack! clack! clack! Clat - ter, clat - ter, clat - ter, clat - ter,

Clat - ter, clat - ter, clat - ter, clat - ter,

Jin - gle, jin - gle, jin - gle, jin - gle, What a mer - ry lay;

Clack! clack! clat - ter, As we dash a - way.

Clat - ter, clat - ter, clat - ter,

*** It may sometimes be convenient to have sleigh-bells to jingle while singing this chorus, and perhaps torpedoes for the crack of the whip, and some device for imitating the clatter of the horses' feet. When this cannot be done, hands and feet may answer the purpose.

S

112 Ring the Bell, Watchman!

H. C. Work.

WITH ENERGY. Published in sheet form by ROOT & CADY. Price 25 cents.

1. High in the bel-fry the old sex-ton stands, Grasp-ing the rope with his
2. Bar - ing his long sil - ver locks to the breeze. First for a mo - ment he
3. Hear! from the hill-top the first sig-nal gun Thun-ders the word that some
4. Bon - fires are blaz-ing and rock-ets as - scend—No mea-ger tri-umph such

thin bo - ny hands: Fix'd is his gaze, as by some mag-ic spell,
drops on his knees, Then with a vig - or that few could ex - cel,
great deed is done; Hear! thro' the val - ley the long ech - oes swell,
to - kens por-tend; Shout, shout! my broth-ers, for "all, all is well!"

Till he hears the dis - tant mur - mur, Ring, ring the bell.
An - swers he the wel - come bid - ding, Ring, ring the bell.
Ev - er and a - non re - peat - ing, Ring, ring the bell.
'Tis the u - ni - ver - sal cho - rus, Ring, ring the bell.

CHORUS.

"Ring the bell, watch-man! ring! ring! ring! Yes, yes! the good news is now on the wing; Yes, yes! they come, and with tid - ings to tell—

Glo - ri - ous and bless - ed tid - ings—Ring, ring the bell!"

The Day is Hot.—Exercise Song.

G. F. R.

ANDANTINO.

1. [1]The day is hot, and we are tired, I wish that we might rest;
2. [2]I stretch my-self—'tis of no use! In - deed it is no sham;
3. [4]The flow - ers in the gar - den fair Bend slow - ly back and forth;
4. [6]O, teach - er, can't we rest a - while? We'll ve - ry qui - et keep;

If teach - er on - ly felt as we, He'd sure - ly think it best.
[3]I nod, and nod, O, dear! O, dear! How sleep - y now I am.
[5]The wind blows round them, and a-bove, In cir - cles flies the moth.
[1]In-deed, I can't make a - ny noise, I'm al - most fast a - sleep!

1 Arms on desk, and head leaning sleepily forward.
2 Stretching.
3 Nodding head sleepily.
4 Move hand (from wrist) left to right.
5 Move hand round and round.
6 Both hands held out to teacher.

Bee Song. G. F. R.

ALLEGRETTO

1. Out in the beau - ti - ful gar - den, Say, will you go with me,
2. Look in the snow - y day - lil - y, Peep in the blue-bell so
3 So in the beau - ti - ful gar - den, Fill - ing the mu - si - cal

now? The o - ri - ole sings as he gai - ly swings
fair; The hon - ey - bee sips with his dain - ty lips
air, The songs in the tree, and the buz - zing bee,

High on the ma - ple bough: Down by the wall of the mead-ow,
Sweet-est of nec - tar there: Deep in the red hon - ey-suck-le,
Wel-come us ev - 'ry where: *Is it* the bird in the ma-ple?

Rows of red hol - ly-hocks see; In ev - er - y one is a
Pois-ing on light wing so free, The hum-ming bird's bill, see it
Is it the hon - ey-bee's hum? Or is it a band from the

CHORUS.

gold-en throne, Throne of the great king bee. Hark! hark! hark!
take its fill, Out of the reach of the bee. Z...................
Fair-y land, Beat-ing a sil - ver drum.

Hear the hum-ming sound, As if a band from Fair-y land, Were

coming from un-der ground: Hark! hark! hark! Hear the buzz and hum,

The Fair - y queen in gold-en sheen, Is beat-ing a sil - ver drum.

Let a divison of the class imitate the buzzing of the bees, by continuing the first part of the sound usually represented by the letter Z, to the tone D, in the chorus. Observe that "Hark" commences exactly with the buzzing, although printed a little after it.

Whistling Farmer boy.

G. F. R.

ALLEGRETTO

1. See the mer - ry far - mer - boy Tramp the mead-ows through;
2. When the far - mer - boy, at noon Rests be - neath the shade,
3. When the bus - y day's em - ploy Ends at dew - y eve,
4. Far - mer - boy is blithe and gay Morn - ing noon or night,

Swing his hoe in care - less joy, While dash - ing off the dew.
List'-ning to the cease-less tune, That's thrill-ing through the glade;
Then the hap - py far - mer - boy Doth haste his work to leave;
Song or glee or roun - de - lay; He's whist-ling with de - light:

Bob - o - link in ma - ples high Trills his notes of glee;
Long and loud the har - vest - fly Winds his bu - gle, 'round:
Trudg - ing down the qui - et vale, Climb - ing o'er the hill,
Mer - ry heart so full of glee, O - ver - full of fun!

Far - mer - boy a gay re - ply, Now whis-tles, cheer - i - ly.
Long, and loud, and shrill and high, He whis-tles back the sound.
Whist - ling back the change-less wail Of plain-tive Whip-poor-will.
Hear him whis - tling mer - ri - ly Un - til the day is done.

Interlude to be whistled.

Piano or Organ.

* Let all who can, whistle this interlude,—both parts, Don't laugh.

Come, Count the time.—Round, in three parts.   G. F. R.

Come, count the time for me, Come, now be - gin:

And you shall quick - ly see, that thus good time we win;

Now, one, two, three, four, one, two, three, four, one, two, three, four, one, two, three.

The Song of the Shoemaker.

1. The shoe-mak-er sat a-mid wax and leath-er, With lap-stone up-on his
2. This hap-py old man was so wise and know-ing, The worth of his time he

knee; Where snug in his shop he de-fied all weath-er, While
know; He bris-tled his ends, and he kept them go-ing, And

draw-ing his quart-ers and sole to-geth-er, A hap-py old man was he.
felt to each mo-ment a stitch was ow-ing, Un-til he got round the shoe.

3. Of every deed that his wax was sealing,
    The closing was firm and fast,
The point of his awl never caused a feeling
Of pain to the toe; and his skill in healing
Was perfect and true to the last.

4. Whenever you gave him a foot to measure,
    With gentle and skillful hand,
He took its proportions with looks of pleasure.
As if you were giving the costliest treasure,
Or making him lord of the land.

5. And many a one did he save from getting
    A fever, a cold, or a cough,
For many a foot did he save from wetting,
When, whether in water or snow 'twas setting,
His shoeing would keep them off.

6. When done with his making at last and mending
    With hope and a peaceful breast;
Resigning his awl, as his thread was ending,
He pass'd from his bench to the grave descending
As high as the king to rest.

1. One bright and pleas-ant sum-mer day, when school was just be-gun,
An i-dle schol-ar stray'd a-way to lin-ger in the sun:

D. C. Come down and buzz a-bout my head, you lit-tle bus-y bee.

Come, lit-tle bird, come down, he said, and sing and play with me;

2. The Robin said, "I cannot play, my nest beneath the blue
Is not half done;" and so away with merry song he flew:
"Nor I," the little busy bee just raised his head to hum,
"Sweet drops of honey wait for me, ah! no, I cannot come."

3. Just then he saw a little ant upon a blade of grass;
"Come now," he said, "don't say you can't, I will not let you pass;
Don't stay upon the earth so brown, come fill me with delight,
. To see you running up and down this daisy, fresh and white "

4. "Ah! no," the little ant replied, "I've so much work to do,
I cannot find the time, beside, to run about with you;
For little ants must work all day to build their tiny home,
Or what would happen to them, pray, when chilly night should come?"

5. "What!" said the little truant boy, "shall bird, and ant and bee,
So busily their time employ, nor stop to play with me,
While I, who know much more than they, spend all my time in fun?
Shall I, alone, at close of day, say I have nothing done?

6. No, no! right back to school I'll go, and let my teacher see
That I my work as well can do as bird, or ant or bee;
And when she tells me, 'Very well!' when she my task has heard,
This story I to her will tell, of bee, and ant and bird."

"Children for the Union."

F. B. Rice.

MARCH TIME

Solo

1. We are
2. We will

one and all for Un - ion, North and South, and East and West; All the
love our land for - ev - er, Dear-est land be-neath the sun; Foe-men's

States in loved com-mu - nion, Heart and hand with free - dom blest.
steel shall not dis - sev - er Youth-ful hearts that now are one.

CHORUS

Then   join   in   the   joy - ful hur - rah,   Hur -

rah for the land of the free; For the Un - ion and peace, for

free - dom and law, Hur - rah for the land of the free.

3. We are all a band of brothers,
   All the States are sisters too,
   And in time there will be others
   That shall happy vows renew.
        CHORUS. Then join, &c.

4. Union now, and Union ever!
   True hearts now for Union all!
   We will keep it safe and never
   Shall our glorious Union fall!
        CHORUS. Then join, &c.

JOYFULLY.

1. Tell it, ye winds, to the far-thest earth, This is the morn of a
2. Who was like him when the storm-cloud burst, And ground the land 'neath a
3. Who was like him when the storm had past, The work of years at an

he - ro's birth; Waft glad the tid - ings from sea to sea,
host ac - curst? When stars of hope in the sky were dim,
end at last? When bow'd all hearts us a wind - swept wood,

CHORUS.

This is a na-tion's great ju - bi - lee. Blest be the day and the
And men's hearts fail'd them, who then like him? Blest, &c.
Who then was like him, the great and good? Blest, &c.

kind - ly sun, That gave to the world a Wash - ing - ton.

School is Done.

1, School is done, school is done! Come and you shall see the fun,
2. Climb the hill with a will; Joy through all our hearts shall thrill,

Let us go, o'er the snow In a mer-ry row.
From the plain, climb a-gain, With our might and main.

Down the hill we rush a-long, Sing-ing loud our
Boys and girls, Oh, join our chime! Shout Hur-ra! for

mer-ry song; School is done, school is done, Come and see the fun.
Win-ter-time; Climb the hill, with a will; Joy our hearts shall thrill!

The Burlesque Band.—Exercise Song. G. F. R.

O, we can play on the Big Base Drum, and this is the mu - sic

to it: Rig, jig, boong is the Big Base Drum, and that is the way we

do it. O, we can play on the Bu - gle Horn, and

this is the mu - sic to it: Tan, tan - ta - rah is the

Bu - gle Horn, and rig, jig, boong is the Big Base Drum, and

that is the way we do it. O, we can play on the

Doub - le Base, and this is the mu - sic to it: Zoo, zoo, zoo is the

Doub - le Base, and tan, tan - ta - rah is the Bu - gle Horn, and

rig, jig, boong is the Big Base Drum, and that is the way we

do it. O, we can play on the Tam - bour - ine, and

this is the mu - sic to it: Jing, a jing, a jing is the

Tam - bour - ine, and zoo, zoo, zoo is the Doub - le Base, and

tan, tan - ta - rah is the Bu - gle Horn, and rig, jig, boong is the

Big Base Drum, and that is the way we do it. O,

we can play on the Old Ban - jo, and this is the music

The Burlesque Band.—Concluded.

to   it: Tum, tum, tum   is   the   Old Ban - jo,   and

jing,   a   jing,   a   jing   is   the   Tam - bour - ine,   and

zoo, zoo, zoo   is   the Doub - le Base, and tan, tan - ta - rah   is   the

Bu - gle Horn, and   rig, jig, boong   is   the   Big Base Drum, and

that is the way we do it.   O, we can play on the Castanet, and this is the music
to it: Tick, tick, i tack is the Castanet, and tum, tum, tum is the Old Banjo, and
jing, a jing, a jing is the Tambourine, and zoo, zoo, zoo is the Double Base, and
tan, tan-ta-rah is the Bugle Horn, and rig, jig, boong is the Big Base Drum, and
that is the way we do it.   O, we can play on the Kettle Drum, and this is the
music to it: Prrrum,* pum, pum is the Kettle Drum, and tick, tick, i tack is the
Castanet, and tum, tum, tum is the Old Banjo, and jing, a jing, a jing is the
Tambourine, and zoo, zoo, zoo is the Double Base, and tan, tan-ta-rah is the
Bugle Horn, and rig, jig, boong is the Big Base Drum, and that is the way we
do it.   O, we can play on the Octave Flute, and this is the music to it: Tootle,
tootle, toot is the Octave Flute, and prrrum, pum, pum is the Kettle Drum, and
tick, tick, i tack is the Castanet, and tum, tum, tum is the Old Banjo, and jing,
a jing, a jing is the Tambourine, and zoo, zoo, zoo is the Double Base, and tan,
tan-ta-rah is the Bugle Horn and rig, jig, boong is the Big Base Drum, and that
is the way we do it.

☞ Observe, that the tune is printed in full once through, and commenced a second time, after
which it goes on in two parts. It is believed that not only the player can continue all the parts,
but that the singers can go on perfectly well, where the words alone are printed. Make such
motions as will be appropriate to each instrument mentioned, and vary the strength of the voice,
also, to suit the character of each. Perhaps the boys may be trusted to beat on the desk with the
soft part of the fist for the *Big Base Drum.*

* Roll the r, in "Prrrum."

Wishes.

G. F. R. 127

1. Don't you wish you were a bird? I do, I do; Fly-ing in the air a - bove? I do, I do; Glad my voice should e'er be heard, If I could but be a bird.

2. Don't you wish you were a cloud? I do, I do; Sail-ing o - ver peo-ple's heads? I do, I do; Wind blow soft, or wind blow loud, I'd not care were I a cloud.

3. Don't you wish you were a flower?
I do, I do;
Perfumed like an angel's wing?
I do, I do:
I'd look fresher ev'ry shower,
If I could but be a flower.

"The Answer."

1. No, I would not be a bird;
Not I, not I;
I don't want to "fly above,"
Not I, not I:
My glad voice can now be heard,
Even though I'm not a bird.

2. I've no wish to be a cloud;
Not I, not I:
For since I'm not thinly clad;
Not I, not I:
Wind blow soft, or wind blow loud,
I don't care to be a cloud.

3. I've no wish to be a flower;
Not I, not I;
Though they're perfumed sweet and rare;
Not I, not I:
Childhood's prayer to Heaven's great power,
Smells more sweet than perfumed flower.

9

The play Ground.

G. F. R.

RECITANDO

1. Wea - ry of play - ing at hide-and-seek,   One of the par - ty who yet could speak, Lean'd
2. Five-year-old Dick from the clover sprang,   "A new pop - gun that will go bang! bang! A

gravely back 'gainst a gateway post, And asked each one, "What he wished for most."
bright tin sword, and a painted drum; And then, I say, let the reb - els come."

3. "I'd like" said Johnny, "a conch and four
   To | dash around to the hotel door;
   That | boys like me, in the street at play,
   Would | have to run, as I ran to-day."

4. Harry, whose eyes had a starry look,
   Smiled | thoughtfully upward, " A great, new
       book |
   Larger than father's great Review,
   That | one might read and never read through."

5. " I wish" said Ernest "I had a ship,"
   "And | I" said Charlie "a nice long whip;"
   Ned | slyly pulled at his neighbor's cuff
   And asked | 'If the master's was long
       enough?'"

6. Herbert wished most for a bat and ball |
   Howard, that the school bells would never
       call; |
   Allen who hides in a thunder storm,
   Longed for a sword and a uniform.

7. The boy 'gainst the gateway post reclined,
   Said | none were just of his turn of mind;
   He only wished of the kindly fates
   A | new hand-sled and a pair of skates.

8. A poor little errand boy passing by |
   Loitered and listened and heaved a sigh ; |
   "These pretty things would be nice
       indeed,
   But I | only wish I could learn to read. "

Be you to Others.—ROUND, IN THREE PARTS.

Be you to oth - ers kind and true; And al - ways

un - to oth - ers do; As you'd have oth - ers do to you.

1. There flowed a lit-tle troubled stream, Re-joic-ing on its way;
2. Ah! then he screamed with might and main, And frighten'd all the trout;
3. "Ho! here's a craft with drip-ping sail! How ma-ny fish to day?"

And naugh-ty Jam-ie closed his book And sly-ly ran a-way;
He would not run a-way a-gain If ev-er he got out;
"I say, young di-ver where's the whale? I guess he's run a-way;"

And bend-ing o'er to watch and wait, With line and crook-ed pin;
A shout a-rose a-long the path, The school was just dis-missed;
"Trans-gres-sors' ways are al-ways hard" The Teach-er said, "to-day;

His hopes sank low-er than his bait, He stum-bled, tum-bled in.
When up came Jam-ie from his bath With line a-round his waist.
We see the tru-ant boy's re-ward, Ah! Jam-ie, does it pay?"

DON'T YOU SEE ME COMING!

G. F. R.

ALLEGRETTO VIVACE. [By permission of H. Tolman & Co, Boston.]

1. Don't you see me com - ing, com - ing,
2. I've been wink - ing, blink-ing, prink-ing,
3. Bob - o' - Link - um, Link - um, Xink-um,

com - ing right a - long? Here's the lit - tle grass - y mead - ow,
ev - er since the morn, Wait - ing for the men to go, and
all in black and gold, We must have our break-fast soon, or

now I'll sing my song. I am Mis - ter Bob - o' Link - um,
leave that field of corn. Blit - sey Lee - dle's wait - ing, too, but
I shall have to scold. Pret - ty lit - tle Blit - sey Lee - dle,

that I s'pose you know, Blit - sey Lee - dle is my wife, she's
nev - er makes a sound, She's a mod - est lit - tle thing, and
sit - ting on the nest, Thinks if she takes care the house that

130

in the grass be - low, yes, yes, yes, Don't you see me com - ing, com - ing,
wears a rus - set gown, yes, yes, yes, Don't you see me com - ing, com - ing,
I can do the rest, yes, yes, yes, Don't you see me go - ing, go - ing,

com-ing right a-long? Here's the lit - tle grass-y mead-ow, where my folks be - long.
com-ing right a-long? Here's the lit - tle grass-y mead-ow, where my folks be - long.
go - ing right a-long? There's a chance, the men are off, and so I'll stop my song.

The Grammar Lesson.

G. F. R,

ALLEGRETTO

1. Three lit - tle words you of - ten see, The ar - ti - cles, a, an, and the:
2. The ad - jec - tives de - cide the noun, As great, small, pret - ty, white, or brown:
3. Verbs tell of some-thing be - ing done, To read, write, count, sing, jump, or run:
4. Con-junc-tions join the words we use, As men and wo - men, boots or shoes:
5. The in - ter - jec - tion shows sur - prise, As, Oh! how pret - ty! Ah! how wise!

A noun's the name of an - y - thing, A school, or gar - den, hoop or swing.
In-stead of nouns the pro-nouns stand, His head, her face, my arm, your hand.
How things are done, the ad - verbs tell, As slow - ly, quick - ly, ill, or well.
The pre - po - si - tions stand be - fore A noun, as in, or through a door.
The whole are called nine parts of speech, Which Read-ing, Writ - ing, Speak-ing teach.

Over the Snow.

B. S. Taylor.

1. O - ver the o - cean of bright spark - ling snow,
2. Un - der a can - o - py gemmed with the light,
3. Min - gling our sing - ing with jing - ling of bells,

Mer - ri - ly O, mer - ri - ly O, Swift as a bird in its
Mer - ri - ly O, mer - ri - ly O, Speed we a - way on our
Mer - ri - ly O, mer - ri - ly O, O - ver the val - ley our

flight we go, Mer - ri - ly, mer - ri - ly O.
path - way bright, Mer - ri - ly, mer - ri - ly O.
mu - sic swells, Mer - ri - ly, mer - ri - ly O.

CHORUS.

Mer - ri - ly, mer - ri - ly O, Mer - ri - ly, mer - ri - ly O;

Swift-ly we go, Mer - ri - ly, mer - ri - ly O.

O-ver the snow..............

By and By.

G. F. R.

MODERATO.

1. These are words so mis-chief mak-ing, That they set the world a - wry;
2. Here's the task for re - ci - ta-tion, Quick-ly con-quer'd with "I'll try;"
3. From the hem-ming and the stitch-ing, Nel - lie turns a - way her eye,
4. Ah! the plea is a de - ceiv-er, Work-ing e - vil on the sly;

When a no - ble un - der - tak - ing, Meets its death in "by and by;"
But the thief, pro - cras - ti - na - tion, False-ly whis-pers "by and by;"
Breath-ing o'er a book, be-witch-ing, "I can do it by and by;"
Wis - dom is an un - be - liev - er, In the faith of "by and by;"

"By and by, by and by," Meets its death in "by and by."
"By and by, by and by," False-ly whis-pers "by and by."
"By and by, by and by," I can do it by and by."
"By and by, by and by," In the faith of "by and by."

Ready for Duty.

ALLEGRETTO.

1. A Daf - fy - down - dil - ly came up in the cold, Through
2. But Daf - fy - down - dil - ly had heard un - der - ground, The
3. "Now then," mur - mur'd Daf - fy, deep down in her heart, "It's
4. There was snow all a - bout her— grey clouds o - ver - head— The

all the brown mold, Thro' all the brown mold, Al - tho' the March breez - es blew
sweet rush - ing sound, The sweet rush - ing sound Of the streams, as they burst off their
time I should start, It's time I should start!" So she push'd her soft wings thro' the
trees all look'd dead, The trees all look'd dead; Then how do you think Daf - fy-

keen on her face, Al - tho' the white snow lay on ma - ny a place.
white win - ter chains—Of the whis-tling spring winds and the pat - ter - ing rains.
hard fro - zen ground, Quite up to the sur - face, and then she look'd round.
down-dil - ly felt, When the sun would not shine and the ice would not melt?

5. "Cold weather!" thought Daffy, still working away,
"The earth's hard to day!
There's but half an inch of my leaves to be seen,
And two-thirds of that is more yellow than green!

6. "I can't do much yet; but I'll do what I can:
It's well I began!
For, unless I can manage to lift up my head,
The people will think that the Spring herself's dead."

7. So, little by little, she brought her leaves out,
All clustered about;
And then her bright flowers began to unfold,
Till Daffy stood robed in her spring green and gold.

8. O, Daffy-down-dilly, so brave and so true!
That I were like you!
So ready for duty in all sorts of weather,
And holding forth courage and beauty together.

Forest Echoes.

ALLEGRETTO

1. A - long the path of the dim old for - est, I stray'd in the dew - y dawn: And
2. They stir'd my heart with their low sweet voi - ces, Like chimes of a ho - lier land: As
3. They float - ed down thro' the list - 'ning si - lence, Like tones of a sil - ver dream; From
4. And ev - er - more, thro' the si - lent march - es, Where life's bu - sy mo - ments throng, I

heard far a - way in the si - lent shad - ows The ech - oes of the morn:
tho' far a - way mid the si - lent branch - es, Were a hap - py angel band:
realms far a - way where there was no sor - row, By life's un - ruf - fled stream:
hear far a - way in the qui - et shad - ows, Those bliss - ful notes of song:

ff   pp   ff   pp

Hark! ech - o sweet! Hark! ech - o sweet! Once a - gain re - ply! Once a - gain re - ply!

ff   pp   ff   pp   ff   pp

Ech - o! Ech - o! Ech - o! Ech - o! Ech - o! sweet good bye! Ech - o sweet good bye!

If convenient let two clear, true, voices in another room imitate the echo singing the notes marked *pp*. In the last line let the echo commence a little before the chorus finish the last note.

The Soldier's Motherless Daughter. U. B. M.

TENDERLY.

1. Let me kiss you, fa - ther, kiss you, I am
2. Must I be a sol - dier's daugh - ter? Does that
4. Oh! my moth - er is in heav - en, Where the

ver - y tired of play; I shall have no one to
mean, I must not cry, When I know that you are
gates have pearl - y bars; And I some - times think I

love me, When my fa - ther goes a - way; For my
go - ing, When I kiss you this good - bye? When you
see her, In the fair - est of the stars; For I

lit - tle pray'r at e - ven, At your knee is al - ways
ride in - to the bat - tle, With the fore - most of your
know she is an an - gel, And, dear fa - ther, don't you

said; And I dream of you till morn - ing, On my
men, Will you think of lit - tle Min - nie? Will you
cry, If I go with her to heav - en, When I

CHORUS.

lit - tle trun - dle bed. I shall have no arms to
want to see her then. I shall, &c.
kiss you this good bye. I shall have no one to

· rest in, I shall have no place to pray, I shall
love me, I shall have no heart to play, So I'll

have no one to love me, When my fa - ther goes a - way.
ask our Heaven-ly Fa - ther To be near you ev - ery day.

Windows to the Sunrise.

G. F. R.

RECITANDO

1. If you want to see the light of the dawn, When it tips with
2. If you want a home where mu - sic-bells ring, Where the heart with
3. If you want to see that beau - ti - ful gleam, When it spans the

pur - ple the hills of morn; When it wreaths the moun-tains in
glad - ness and joy doth sing; Where the gold - en mo-ments roll
mead-ows of life's fair dream; If you want the sun-shine of

flee - cy curls, And sparkles the mead-ows with dew - y pearls. You must
sweet - ly round With nev - er a mur-mur or jar - ring sound. You must
joy to stay, And rest on your path like a sweet June day. You must

sleep in a room with win - dows With win - dows to the sun - rise,
live in a house with win - dows With win - dows to the sun - rise,
have in your heart some win - dows That o - pen to the sun - rise,

You must sleep in a room With win-dows to the sun - rise.
You must live in a house With win-dows to the sun - rise.
You must have in your heart Some win-dows to the sun - rise.

Free! Free! Free!

G. F. R.

WITH ENERGY.

1. Free! Free! Free! Shall all our coun - try be, With
2. Free! Free! Free! Our speech shall ev - er be, Far
3. Free! Free! Free! Our thoughts shall ev - er be, Yes,

out a lash, with - out a chain; With - out re-proach with -
as earth's wa - ters run and ring; Far as the wild - birds
free - er yet with ev - 'ry year; What man may dare, a

out a stain: We'll shout from sea to sea, Free! for - ev - er free!
soar and sing: We'll shout from sea to sea, Free! for - ev - er free!
heart holds dear: We'll shout from sea to sea, Free! for - ev - er free!

1. Jip - i - dee! Jip - i - dee! blithe and gay, Oh, but he can pipe a
2. Nim-ble Dick! Nim-ble Dick! black and tan, Keep the lit - tle ras - cal
3. Ba - by Bun! Ba - by Bun! great blue eyes, Look-ing now so cun-ning,

mer - ry round - e - lay; Jip - i - dee! Jip - i - dee! sweet - ly sing,
qui - et, if you can; Here he is, there he is, don't you see
now so ver - y wise, Frol-ick-ing, chir-rup-ing, full of fun;

Bird - ie of the gold - en wing: Morn-ing bright brings his song so free;
What a bus - y dog is he? Coat as sleek as a dan-dy's clothes,
What a jol - ly Ba - by Bun! Fat, round face, and a dim-pled chin,

Soft at night hear his chee, chee, chee; Jip - i - dee, Jip - i - dee,
Proud is Dick of his ta - per nose; Here he is, there he is,
Three white teeth and a rogu - ish grin, Frol-ick-ing, chir-rup-ing,

sweet - ly sing, Bird - ie of the gold - en wing.
don't you see What a bus - y dog is he?
full of fun; What a jol - ly Ba - by Bun.

A Fair Little Girl.

G. F. R.

MODERATO.

1. A fair lit - tle girl sat un - der a tree, And
2. A num - ber of rooks came o - ver her head; All
3. The hors - es they neighed, the ox - en, too, lowed, And

sewed just as long as her eyes could see, Then smooth'd down her work and
cry-ing, "Caw! caw!" on their way to bed; She said, as she watch'd their
gen-tly the sheep's bleat came down the road, All seem - ing to say with

fold - ed it right, And mur-mur'd, "Dear work, good night! good night!"
cu - ri - ous flight, "O, lit - tle black things, good night! good night!"
qui - et de - light, "O, good lit - tle girl, good night! good night!"

ALLEGRETTO.   Published in sheet form by ROOT & CADY.   Price 35 cents.

1. There's a coun-try fam'd in sto - ry, As you've of - ten-times been
2. Once a man in An-dros - cog-gin, Or in some out-land - ish
3. Then he cross'd the roll-ing prai-ries, Stretch-ing on-ward like the
4. Climb-ing o'er the Rock-y moun-tains, On he kept his wea - ry

told; 'Tis a land of might - y riv - ers, Run - ning
place, With a view to find this coun - try, To the
sea; "I am bound to find this coun - try, If there's
way, Till the broad Pa - ci - fic's wa - ters Right be-

o - ver sands of gold: The a - bode of peace and
west - ward set his face. He was wea - ry at Chi-
such a one," said he: So he swam the Mis - sis-
fore his vis - ion lay: Here he sat him down and

plen - ty, And with qui - et - ness 'tis blest! But this
ca - go, So he sat him down to rest; But 'twas
sip - pi, Then up - on Mis - sou - ri's breast, He ex-
pon - der'd, But for him there was no rest; "'Tis an

coun - try that's so fam - ous   Is   a - way off   in   the   west.
on - ly there the   cen - ter,   Not   the   fa - bled gold - en   west.
plor'd the wilds of   Kan - sas   For   this coun - try   in   the   west.
is - land, sure-ly," said he,   This   fair coun - try   in   the   west.

CHORUS.

'Tis a-way off in the west,   'Tis a - way off in the west;

in the west,   in the west;

O!   I   fear we ne'er shall find it,   'Tis so far off in the west.

5. So a vessel quick he builded,
  And the shore he left behind;
Sailing on with eager longings,
  Still this happy isle to find:
After many days, one morning
  He beheld the wish'd for land;
Steering 'mid the shoals and breakers,
  Quickly reach'd the golden strand.
       CHORUS—

6. From his gallant bark he landed,
  Wading thro' the curling foam,
With his eyes wide ope' with wonder,
  For he found himself at home:
Then he learn'd that one forever
  Might go on and never rest;
Still they would not find this country,
  For 'tis always further west.
       CHORUS—

It will be an excellent plan sometimes to have this sung as a song and chorus. The song by a boy or girl, who can give the story distinctly, and with proper expression.

10

Don't be Vain.

G. F. R.

ALLEGRETTO.

1. Some nice lit - tle hon - ey - bees hap-pen'd, one day, To light where a horn-et was
He drew them up proud-ly, and said," Go a - way! I can - not en-dure you, poor,
2. One chill au-tumn morn-ing the bees heard a sound, So fee - ble and mourn-ful, and
The poor, dy - ing hor - net lay low on the ground; The bees said," Ah! who's a 'plain,

sun - ning his wings;)
plain, com-mon thing!" } The bees did their work, and then gai - ly flew home All
plain-tive and low;)
com-mon thing,' now?" } Don't think you are fine be - cause fine things you wear; Don't

la - den with hon-ey, for drear, win - ter days; The spite - ful young hor-net con-
look with con-tempt on the bu - sy or plain; Some chill au-tumn day you may

tin - ued to roam A - mong the bright lil - ies in in - do-lent plays.
chance to be where You'll have to re - mem - ber your ill words a - gain.

Tiny little Raindrops.

James R. Murray.

ALLEGRETTO

1. Ti - ny lit - tle rain - drops, Fall - ing in the street;
2. Ti - ny lit - tle rain - drops, Bless - ing all the land.
3. Like the ti - ny rain - drops, Mod - est, pure and still;

Tap - ping at my win - dow, Mak - ing mu - sic sweet.
Mes - sen - gers of love, sent By a Fa - ther's hand,
May we - er, trust - ing Do our Fa - ther's will.

How I love to see thee, Glad re - fresh - ing rain, Now
Tell - ing of his good - ness. Sing - ing as they go. Of
Then when we are ris - ing, In His life di - vine, Oh,

bring - ing to the pret - ty flow - ers, Life and Hope a - gain.
light and love, from heaven a - bove us, To the world be - low.
bright - er than the glo - rious rain - bow, Shall our radiance shine.

Have you sold your matches Tom?

G. F. R.

1. Are all your match-es sold yet, Tom?
2. We'll call the sun our fa-ther, Tom,
3. But Oh, there's One a-bove him, Tom,
4. We'll tell Him all our sor-rows, Tom,

Are all your match-es done? Then let us to the
We'll call the sun our mother; We'll call each pleas-ant
Who loves us more than he; Who made the great bright
We'll tell Him all our care; We'll tell Him where we

o-pen square, And warm us in the sun; To
lit-tle beam, A sis-ter or a brother; He
sun to shine, With beams so warm and free; He
sleep at night, We'll tell Him how we fare; And

warm us in the sweet bright sun, To feel his kin-dling
thinks no shame to kiss us, Tom, Al-though we rag-ged
is our re-al fa-ther, Tom, Al-though while here be-
then, Oh then to cheer us, Tom, He'll send his sun to

glow; For his kind looks are the on - ly looks Of
go; For his kind looks are the on - ly looks Of
low; The sun's kind looks are the on - ly looks Of
glow; For his kind looks are the on - ly looks Of

CHORUS.

friend - ship that we know. O Tom, don't you cry, Al-

though the cold winds blow; For the sun is shin - ing

bright and warm, In the great square down be - low.

ALLEGRETTO

1. We are com - ing sang the rob - ins, For the
2. There's a tree be - neath your win - dow, With a
3. You will scat - ter crumbs it may be, On your

woods and groves are gay, Will you give us kind - ly
par - a - dise of leaves, We will build our rob - in
friend - ly win - dow sill, For each dar - ling rob - in

greet - ing, Lit - tle Jes - sie, Lit - tle May? We will
home - stead, In the branch - es 'neath the eaves, There will
ba - by, Has an emp - ty, gap - ing bill, We will

join your ma - tin car - ols, . We will chant your ves - per
be the sweet - est chirp - ing, In the gar - den by and
give our fare - well con - cert, When the flow - ers pass a -

lay, While we wait your sweet - er ech - oes, Lit - tle
by, When our pleas - ant toil is end - ed, And the
way, But will come a - gain as they will, Lit - tle
CHORUS.
Jes - sie, Lit - tle May, We are com - ing sang the
nest - lings learn to fly, We are com - ing &c.
Jes - sie, Lit - tle May,
rob - ins, For the woods and groves are gay, Will you
give us kind - ly greet - ing, Lit - tle Jes - sie, Lit - tle May?

ALLEGRETTO.

1. Come, O come, and gai - ly go O'er the spark-ling
2. See, the sun - light on the ground Scat - ters dia-monds
3. Crowd - ing, fill - ing all the air, How they float the

ice and snow; On the pond the ska - ters glide,
all a - round; See the ice up - on the trees,
snow - flakes fair; Like ten thou - sand fai - ries white,

Down the hill the coast - ers slide: Hear the sleigh-bells'
Earth has no such gems as these: Hear them sing, in
Dan - cing in their mad de - light: Hear them sing, in

hap - py chime, Win - ter, win - ter, mer - ry time, Hear the sleigh-bells'
tink-ling chime, Win - ter, win - ter, mer - ry time, Hear them sing in
whis-per'd chime, Win - ter, win - ter, mer - ry time, Hear them sing in

hap - py chime, Win - ter, mer - ry, mer - ry time.
tink - ling chime, Win - ter, mer - ry, mer - ry time.
whis - per'd chime, Win - ter, mer - ry, mer - ry time.

Good Night.

G. F. R.

ANDANTINO.

1. Come, let us sing a pleas-ant song, As to our homes we go a-long;
2. We'll seek in peace each qui-et home, For now the evening shades have come;
3. Yes, dear com-pan-ions, fare you well, A-gain our part-ing num-bers swell;

With cheer-ful tones and spir-its light, We'll sing a-gain our glad good-night.
With cheer-ful tones and spir-its light, We'll sing a-gain our glad good-night.
With cheer-ful tones and spir-its light, We sing once more our glad good-night.

REPEAT pp

Good night, good night, good night, good night.

Good night, good night,

Kiss me, Mother, Kiss your Darling.

G. F. R.

TENDERLY.   Published in sheet form by ROOT & CADY.   Price 35 cents.

1. Kiss me, Moth-er, kiss your dar - ling, Lean my head up - on your
2. Kiss me, Moth-er, kiss your dar - ling, Breathe a bless-ing on my
3. O, how dark this world is grow-ing, Hark! I hear the an - gel

breast; Fold   your   lov - ing   arms   a - round   me,
brow;   For   I'll   soon   be   with   the   an - gels,
band: How   I   long   to   join   their   num - ber

I   am   wea - ry,   let   me   rest: Scenes of life   are swift-ly
Faint - er grows my breath e'en now: Tell the lov'd ones not to
In   that fair and hap - py land: Hear you not that heav'n-ly

fad - ing, Bright - er   seems   the   oth - er   shore;
mur - mur, Say   I   died   our   flag   to   save,
mu - sic, Float - ing   near   so   soft   and   low;

I am stand-ing by the riv-er, An-gels wait to waft me o'er.
And that I shall slum-ber sweet-ly In the sol-dier's hon-or'd grave.
I must leave you, fare-well, Moth-er! Kiss me once be-fore I go.

CHORUS.

Kiss me, Moth-er, kiss your dar-ling, kiss your dar-ling, Moth-er,

Fold your lov-ing arms a-
Lean my head up-on your breast, up-on your breast.... O fold your
Fold your lov-ing arms a-

round me,
lov-ing arms a-round me, Moth-er, I am wea-ry, let me rest.
round me,

Throwing the Stone. G. F. R.

RECITANDO.

1. They said I was a naught - y boy, I had not been so
2. I was so sorry that I cried, But when the boys all
3. And then they laughed and ran a - way, And hollowed as they
4. Oh! do not look so grieved, so sad, I never will do

un - til then; But they had taken ev - 'ry toy, And
called me "Cain;" It made me angry, and I tried To
turn'd a - bout, "You'll be a man some dread - ful day, And
so a - gain; I'm sorry that I was so bad, And

call'd away my broth - er Ben, Who bade me go and
throw that very stone a - gain; I want - ed, O! so
set the lake on fire, no doubt;" And then, mam - ma, I
so I've said to broth - er Ben, I know we shall be

play a - lone, And then, mam - ma, I threw the stone.
much just then, To hurt them all as I had Ben.
was so vexed, I did not know what to do next.
friends once more, And love each oth - er as be - fore.

spiritoso.

1. Hur - rah! for the morn - ing of morn - ings has come!
2. Hur - rah! let the lips of the can - nons be red,
3. Hur - rah for our ban - ner! the Flag of the Free,
4. Hur - rah for the Fu - ture! We, boys of the land,

Un - furl ev - 'ry ban - ner, and beat ev - 'ry drum!
In hon - or of he - roes, the liv - ing and dead;
Its star - ry folds float - ing from sea un - to sea;
In Free - dom's grave coun - cils are des - tin'd to stand;

Let bird, boy and bu - gle tell earth, sea and sky,
For those who first taught us to con - quer or die,
Its stripes for the trai - tor, who dares to de - fy,
Then down with the trea - son, whose life is a lie;

'Tis Free - dom's glad birth - day, the Fourth of Ju - ly.
And those who at Vicks - burg kept Fourth of Ju - ly.
Its stars go be - fore us on Fourth of Ju - ly.
And up with the rock - ets, 'tis Fourth of Ju - ly.

WEAVER JOHN.

B. R. H.

1. Down in that cot - tage lives
2. Close by his side is this
3. Pus - sy is frisk - ing a -
4. Soft as the hum of the

Wea - ver John And a hap - py old John is he;
gen - tle wife And she's twirl - ing the flax - en thread;
bout the room, With her kit - tens one, two, three, four;
dame's low wheel, Does the mu - sic of time roll on;

Maud is the name of his dear old dame, And a
Sweet to his ear is the low wheel's hum It was
Tow - ser is tak - ing his want - ed nap On the
Morn - ing and noon of a use - ful life Bring a

CHORUS.

bless - ed old dame is she. Whick - it - y, whack - it - y,
purchased when they were wed. Whick - it - y, &c.
set - tle be - hind the door. Whick - it - y, &c.
peace - ful - ly set - ting su . Whick - it - y, &c.

156

click and clack, How the shut-tles do glance and ring! Here they go,

there they go, forth and back, and a stac - ca - to song they sing.

Little Flow'ret.

B. R. H.

MODERATO

1. Lit - tle flow - 'ret, press thy way, Thro' the dark - ness in - to day:
2. Bee and blos - som, each ful - fills Pur - po - ses our Fa - ther wills;
3. Like the lit - tle flower we press On, to hope, and hap - pi - ness;

Ev - 'ry-thing shall wel-come thee, Warb-ling bird, and bus - y bee.
Chil-dren should not i - dle be, Sav - ior, let us work for thee.
Ev - er in God's pur-pose true, Do - ing all that we can do.

How it Marches.

H. H. H.

WITH ENERGY.

1. How it march - es! the Flag of the Un - ion,
2. Oh! our boys love the Flag of the Un - ion,
3 Sai - lors, too, love the Flag of the Un - ion,

The dear old Flag of the Un - ion, And our
The dear old Flag of the Un - ion, In the
The dear old Flag of the Un - ion, They have

bo - soms swell with pride, While we see it float - ing wide
front of ev - ery fight, 'Mid the bat - tle's lu - rid light,
nailed it firm and fast To the top of ev - 'ry mast,

O - ver all as the Flag of the Un - ion.
They have died for the Flag of the Un - ion.
For their joy is the Flag of the Un - ion.

How it march - es! The Flag of the Un - ion,

The dear old Flag of the Un - ion, It shall

float in pow'r and pride, O - ver all the land so wide,

Ev - er more as the Flag of the Un - ion.

4. Uncle Sam loves the Flag of the Union,
   The dear old Flag of the Union,
   And amid the loss we mourn,
   Says in thunder tones so stern,
   " All shall honor the Flag of the Union."
   How it marches, &c.

11

MODERATO.

1. Now all our work is done, sis-ter school-mates, brother school-mates,
2. Take, take our ear - nest thanks, faith-ful teach-ers, lov-ing teach-ers,
3. Once more we sing to you, gen-tle friends and lov-ing par-ents,

Wel - come Va - ca - tion - time now is draw - ing nigh;
Thanks for each help - ful word, ev - 'ry coun - sel high;
Come oft to cheer us on, as the sea - sons fly;

Rest is sweet when toil is end - ing; Now your cheer - ful
Now be hap - py days be - fore you; Now may sun - ny
Grate - ful - ly we ev - er greet you; Smiles of wel - come

voi - ces blend-ing, Sing, broth-ers, sis - ters all, gai - ly sing good-bye!
skies shine o'er you: Sing, broth-ers, sis - ters all, gai - ly sing good-bye!
al - ways meet you: Sing, broth-ers, sis - ters all, gai - ly sing good-bye!

I would if I could.

A. Craik Smyth. 161

ALLEGRETTO

1. "I would if I could," tho' much it's in use,
2. "Come John," said a school-boy, "now do not re-fuse
3. At the door of a man-sion, a child thin-ly clad,

Is but a mis-tak-en and slug-gish ex-cuse; And
Come solve me this prob-lem you can if you choose," But
While the cold wind blew freely, was beg-ging for bread; A

ma-ny a per-son who could if he would, Is of-ten heard
John at that mo-ment was not in the mood, And yawn-ing-ly
rich man pass'd by her as trem-bling she stood, He answered her

say-ing, "I would if I could"
answered "I would if I could"
cold-ly, "I would if I could"

4. The scholar receiving his teacher's advice,
The swearer admonished to quit such a vice
The child when requested to try to be good
Oft gives the same answer "I would if I
could."

5. But if we may credit what good people say,
That where a strong will is, there's always
a way
And whatever ought to be can be and should,
We never need utter "I would if I could."

ANDANTINO. Published in sheet form by Roor & Cady. Price 30 cents.

1. 'Twas down in the mead - ows, the vio - lets were blow - ing,
2. Her eyes soft and ten - der, the vio - lets out - vie - ing,
3. The bright flow'rs are fad - ed, the young grass has fall - en,

And the spring - time grass was fresh and green; And the
And a fair - er form was nev - er seen; With her
And a dark cloud hov - ers o'er the scene; For the

birds by the brook - let their sweet songs were sing - ing,
brown silk - en tress - es, her cheek like the ros - es,
death an - gel took her, and left me in sor - row,

When I first met my dar - ling Dai - sy Deane.
There was none like my dar - ling Dai - sy Deane.
For my lost one, my dar - ling Dai - sy Deane.

CHORUS.
Repeat after last verse *pp.*

None knew thee but to love thee, thou dear one of my heart,

O, thy mem - 'ry is ev - er fresh and green;

ev - er fresh and

Tho' the sweet buds may with - er, and fond hearts be bro - ken,

green, the sweet

Still I'll love thee, my dar - ling Dai - sy Deane.

4. O, down in the meadows I still love to wander,
Where the young grass grew so fresh and green;
But the bright golden visions of springtime have faded
With the flowers, and my darling Daisy Deane.
CHORUS—

Resisting the Tempter.

MODERATO.

1st voice. 1. Come, mer - ry lad, I am wait - ing for you;
" 2. Come, mer - ry lad, take a seat by my side;
" 3. Come, mer - ry lad, take a walk, and we'll find
" 4. Walk - ing, and rid - ing and row - ing, for you,

Come, take a sail on the wa - ter so blue.
Po - ny is pranc - ing, I'll give you a ride.
Where swing the ma - ple blooms, red, in the wind.
Must they all wait 'till the school hours are through?

2d voice. Dear - ly I love on the riv - er to row,
" Dear - ly i love a gay gal - lop, you know;
" Dear - ly I love where the spring - blos - soms grow;
" Yes, and I'll go 'till the last hour is done!

Blithe is the boat, but to school I must go.
Po - ny trots well, but to school I must go.
Ram - bling is fine, but to school I must go.
Then, boys, hur - rah for the play and the fun.

CHORUS.

Brave lit - tle he - ro, well done, well done for you!

Thus will we an - swer the wi - ly tempt - er, too.

[The chorus take up the words of the 2d voice in every verse when they get here.]

Dear - ly I love on the riv - er to row;

Blithe is the boat, but to school I must go.

O come away to the School-Room.

H. R. Palmer.

ALLEGRETTO

1. O come a - way to the school-room, O come quick-ly a - way;
2. Now play claims all our at - ten - tion, With joy mer - ri - ly shout!
3. And when our stud-ies are o - ver, We'll hie a-way to our homes;

'Tis there pleas - ure and hap - pi-ness wait us, Come quick - ly a-
We play just as we work, with a will; and All mer - ri - ly
O yes, joy - ful - ly haste we a - way to Home, bright, hap - py

FINE

way. There our teach - ers so kind and o - blig - ing,
shout. When the bell with its ring - ing re - calls us,
home. There our pa - rents so kind - ly will greet us,

Help us our tasks to ful - fill, And with kind - ness and
Glad - ly the sound we o - bey; Take our seats, and to
Ask if our les-sons are learned. With what pleas - ure then,

D. C.

love for each oth - er, Joy each bo - som shall thrill,
stud - y ad - dress us For the rest of the day.
will we re - peat them, And mer - it the an - swer "well done."

Tweet! Tweet! Tweet!

W. J. R.

ALLEGRETTO.

1. Tweet! tweet! tweet! Sings a bird in the tree With his
2. Tweet! tweet! tweet! Sings the bird in the tree To his
3. Tweet! tweet! tweet! Sings the bird in the tree, For he
4. Tweet! tweet! tweet! Sings the bird in the tree, Both his

voice and his dear lit - tle heart full of glee;
mate, and he tells her how hap - py they'll be;
thinks that near hatch'd all those white eggs should be;
mate's and his own heart are now full of glee;

Tweet! tweet! tweet! So he sings all the day, And when
Tweet! tweet! tweet! And they build at their nest, Where with-
Tweet! tweet! tweet! And he scarce - ly has said, When from
Tweet! tweet! tweet! They have no more to say; But in

night's shad - ows come to his nest flies a - way.
in a few days nice white eggs soft - ly rest.
each brok - en shell peeps a feath - er - less head.
au - tumn both they and their young fly a - way.

OCEAN BLUE.

G. F. R.

MODERATO.

1. My moth-er's cot was by the sea,
2. I had a boat, a tin - y craft,
3. And I tho't of cit - ies grand and old,

And I heard the break-ers roar, In the calm sweet dawn of a
Like an In-dian's birch ca - noe; And it float - ed off on a
And of won-ders strange and new; As I saw the ships with their

sum-mer's morn, A - way on the o - cean shore; In the
bright May morn, A - way on the o - cean blue; And it
snow - y wings, Sail o - ver the o - cean blue; As I

calm sweet dawn of a sum - mer's morn, A - way on the o - cean
seem'd to say, as it danc'd a - way, "I'm off on the o - cean
saw them sail on the flow - ing gale, Far o - ver the o - cean

168

shore; A - way, a - way, a - way, A - way, a - way, a - way, A-
blue; A - way, a - way, a - way, A - way, a - way, a - way, A-
blue; A - way, a - way, a - way, A - way, a - way, a - way, A-

A - way.................. A - way..................

way, a - way, a - way, a - way, a - way on the o - cean shore.
way, a - way, a - way, a - way, a - way on the o - cean blue.
way, a - way, a - way, a - way, a - way o'er the o - cean blue.

The Three Rabbits.

G. F. R.

RECITANDO.

1. Three young rab-bits came one day, When the leaves were bud-ding out;
2. But while play-ing came a - long Sports-men, each with mur-d'rous gun;
3. When the rab-bits saw the men Point - ing at them with the guns,
4. One stopp'd star-ing, and got shot, One popp'd quick-ly out of sight;
5. Take due no - tice from these three, Home's the saf-est place of all;

From their win - ter holes to play, And they ran and frisk'd a - bout.
Think-ing sure it was no wrong To take aim at all or one.
Each glanc'd once at them, and then Each but one was prov'd a dunce.
One rush'd where the guns were not, But was trapp'd and held there tight.
Who will there from dan - ger flee Will not in - to spring-traps fall.

ANDANTINO

1. This Bol - ter Brook is a beau - ti - ful brook While the
2. You launch your boat on the per - i - lous tide, With a
3. There is a boy that I hap - pen to know, Ver - y
4. He comes to school at the nine o -'clock bell, And he

A - pril rains do pour; But when the rain stops, His courage all drops
will the oars to try, The foam and the spray, All van-ish a - way
much like Bol-ter Brook, As read-y a lad As need to be had,
real - ly means to try; But when the bell stops, His courage all drops,

And Bol - ter is no more. Oh the long pull, and the strong pull, No
And leave you high and dry. Oh the long pull, &c.
But will not mind his book. Oh the long pull, &c.
And leaves him high and dry. Oh the long pull, &c.

mat - ter. what's the weath - er, Is the - glo - rious way to crown the day and we'll all march on to - geth - er, Is the

glo-rious way to crown the day and we'll all march on to - geth - er.

Sowing Seed.—EXERCISE SONG.

G. F. R.

ALLEGRETTO

1. Now the Far - mer sows his seed, [4]Up and [5]down, [2]here and [3]there
2. Soon the ten - der blades of [1]grain [2]Right and [3]left [4]up will [5]spring.

O - ver all the lev - el mead; [1]Right and [2]left, [6]ev-'ry where.
Mak - ing glad the smil - ing plain, [1]Fling the [2]seed, far-mer, [6]fling.

1 Move right hand gently to and fro.   **4** Both hands up.
2 Right hand to the right.   **5** Both hands down.
8 Left hand to the left.   **6** Close hands with a clap.

Lillie of the Snow-Storm.

Henry C. Work.

WITH EXPRESSION—*not too fast.*   Published in sheet form by ROOT & CADY.   Price 30 cts.

1. To his home, his once white, once lov'd cot - tage, Late at
2. Far a - cross the prai - rie stood a dwell - ing, Where from
3. Lil - lie prays— the harps are hush'd in Heav - en— An - gels
4. Morn - ing dawns— the hus - band and the fa - ther, So - ber'd

night, a poor in - e - briate came; To his wife, the wait - ing wife and
harm they oft had found re - treat; Thith - er now, all brave and un - com
poise them mid - way in the sky; Up from earth there comes a wail of
now, to seek his flock has come; Lil - lie dear is liv - ing, but her

daugh - ter, Who for him had fann'd the mid - night flame: Rude - ly
plain - ing, Did they urge their wea - ry, way - worn feet: But their
sor row, Such a wail as must be heard on High: "Fa - ther,
moth - er— Hours a - go, an au - gel bore her home: Ah, poor

met, they an - swer'd him with kind - ness—Gave him all their own un - tast - ed
strength, un - e - qual to their cour - age, Fail'd them as they wan - der'd to and
dear! my oth - er, bet - ter Fa - ther! Won't you hear your daugh - ter Lil - lie
man! how bit - ter is his an - guish, As he now re - pents his pun - ish'd

store; 'Twas but small, and he with aw-ful curs-es, Spurn'd the
fro; Till, at last, the fee-ble, faint-ing moth-er, Speech less
pray! Won't you send some strong and care-ful an - gel, Who will
sin, Bend-ing o'er the child, who, half un-con-scious, Sad - ly

CHORUS.

gift, and drove them from his door. While the storm, the wild, wild win-try
sank up - on the drift-ed snow. While the storm, &c.
help my moth-er on her way." While the storm, &c.
cries, "Please, fa-ther, let us in!" While the storm, &c.

tem-pest, Swept a-cross the prai-ries cold and white; What a

shame that Lil-lie and her moth-er Were a-broad on such a fear-ful night!

1. Now Kit - tie and Nell, I've some-thing to tell, Just
2. The same dar - ling bird, you of - ten have heard 'Mid
3. They'd five lit - tle chicks, the ti - ni - est bits Of
4. At last, grown and strong, the moth - er bird's song, Each
5. But ah! bye and bye, the win - ter drew nigh, The
6. Ah! sad was their flight, the ground was all white With

look from the win-dow with me, Come gent - ly; now hush, and
ap - ple blooms, close by the wall, When build - ing a nest, where
bird - ies that ev - er you saw, Who quar-relled and ate, both
nest - ling en - ticed from its home. She taught them with care, to
'blos -soms were fa - ded and dead, Our rob - in flock too, their
frost, and the sharp sting-ing sleet; But then with the show'rs, and

hear the sweet gush Of the rob - in that swings in the tree.
soft they might rest, She lived with her mate 'till the fall.
ear - ly and late, 'Till feath - er'd from bill un - to claw.
cleave the blue air, And fear - less for in - sects to roam.
wings spread a - new For lands to which sum - mer had fled.
up-spring-ing flow'rs, They're com-ing, the spring-time to greet.

Hear the wild trill! it leaps like a rill, Mu-si-cal li-quid and

clear. Whis-tle and sing, thou bird of the spring, The

days of the sum-mer are near.

12

QUEEN OF MAY.

G. F. R.

ALLEGRETTO.

1. Come to the wood-lands, a - way, a - way;
2. Down in the mead - ow, be - yond the brook,
3. Come to the lawn, and thine heart shall flow
4. Beau - ti - ful one! as the sun - rays fall

Gath - er its blooms for our Queen of May; Ev - 'ry - thing love - ly and
Blos - soms are spread like an o - pen book; Rev - 'rent - ly gath - er each
Out in a dream of its long a - go; Snows of the years that thy
O - ver each tress, and thy cor - o - nal; Ev - er may bless - ings of

bright and rare, Wreathe in a gar - land for one so fair;
pearl - y gem; One who hath loved us hath cared for them:
locks have kissed, Float - ing a - way as a moun - tain mist:
life de - scend, Light - ing thy path to its far - ther end:

Sing with the wild - bird a song to - day, Lil - lie, our Lil - lie, is
Heav - en is wear ing a smile to - day, Lil - lie, our Lil - lie, is
Join in the song and the dance to - day, Lil - lie, our Lil - lie, is
Thou hast a throne in the heart to - day, Lil - lie, sweet Lil - lie, our

Queen of May, Lil - lie, our Lil - lie, is Queen of May.
Queen of May, Lil - lie, our Lil - lie, is Queen of May.
Queen of May, Lil - lie, our Lil - lie, is Queen of May.
Queen of May, Lil - lie, sweet Lil - lie, our Queen of May.

Excursion Song.

B. B. H.

ALLEGRETTO.

1. Ho! ho! ho! Out to the beau - ti - ful groves we go;
2. Sing! sing! sing! Heav - en shall smile at the praise we bring;
3. Play! play! play! Run, oh, ye hap - py ones while ye may;

This is our hol - i - day now, you know; Sweet shall our mel - o - dies
For - est and mead - ow with mu - sic ring, Ech - o the cad - en - ces
Roam thro' the for - ests at will to - day, Pour-ing your shouts and your

float and flow, Out on the balm - y air:
grace - fully fling. Out on the balm - y air:
laugh - ter gay, Out on the balm - y air:

Bear them, ye breez-es that gen - tly blow, Scat - ter them ev - 'ry-
Bear them a - loft on her sil - v'ry wing, Scat - ter them ev - 'ry-
Syl - vi - a beck-ons, oh speed a - way, Scat - ter them ev - 'ry-

where; Bear them, ye breez - es that gen - tly blow,
where; Bear them a - loft on her sil - v'ry wing,
where; Syl - vi - a beck - ons, oh speed a - way,

gen - tly blow, gen - tly blow; Bear them, ye breez - es that
sil - v'ry wing, sil - v'ry wing; Bear them a - loft on her
speed a - way, speed a - way; Syl - vi - a beck - ons, oh

gen - tly blow, Scat - ter them ev - 'ry - where.
sil - v'ry wing, Scat - ter them ev - 'ry - where.
speed a - way, Scat - ter them ev - 'ry - where.

The Young Temperance Volunteer. J. R. Murray. 179

ALLEGRETTO.

1. I'm go-ing to en-list, boys, I'm go-ing to en-list,
   'Tis not the south-ern reb-els, Nor yet a for-eign foe;
2. 'Tis wine, and beer and ci-der, And glit-ter-ing cham-pagne;
   We'll fight un-til we con-quer En-list-ing for the war;
3. Ah! 'tis no worth-less treas-ure We save from ut-ter doom;
   Oh! 'tis a glo-rious strug-gle, For tem-per-ance and truth;
4. We'll nev-er mind the hard-ships, Nor self-de-ni-al fear;
   We need not ask for boun-ty, Nor think of wa-ges now;

To fight the ug-liest en-emy That ev-er did ex-ist:
But trai-tors at the hearth-stone We'll smite with dead-ly blow.
'Tis rum, and gin and bran-dy, With all their hid-eous train:
And cry, "Ex-ter-mi-na-tion," From hence-forth ev-er-more.
'Tis health, and wealth and rea-son, Joys now and joys to come:
Come, boys, give it our strength now, The vig-or of our youth.
Hard ser-vice does not hurt us, But makes our worth ap-pear:
For by and by a bright crown Shall grace each vic-tor's brow.

CHORUS.

Hur-rah! hur-rah for tem-per-ance! Who would not fight for tem-per-ance?

Come, join the ranks, fall in-to line, And march to vic-to-ry!

ANDANTINO.

1. Row! row! row! O - ver the beau - ti - ful blue we go! Row! Row!
2. Row! row! row! O - ver the beau - ti - ful blue we go! Row! Row!
3. Row! row! row! O - ver the beau - ti - ful blue we go! Row! Row!

Row! Row! O - ver the wa - ters we go, Light - ly ev - 'ry
Row! Row! O - ver the wa - ter we go, Star - ry vaults a -
Row! Row! O - ver the wa - ters we go, Heart to heart we'll

heart is bound-ing Gay the voice of song is sound-ing
bove us beam-ing Star - ry depths be - low us seem-ing
sail to - geth - er Hand in hand for aye and ev - er

Sweet the light gui - tar re - sound-ing; Thus we gai - ly
Sil - ver wave - lets round us gleam-ing, Thus we gai - ly
Naught shall change us naught shall sev - er, Thus we gai - ly

row,   Thus we gai-ly row,   Thus we gai-ly row.
row,   Thus we gai-ly row,   Thus we gai-ly row.
row,   Thus we gai-ly row,   Thus we gai-ly row.

Tic, Tic.

W. J. R

1. Tic! Tic! Tic! Tic! Stead - i - ly the clock goes on
2. Tic! Tic! Tic! Tic! When at morn we gath - er here
3. Tic! Tic! Tic! Tic! Anx - ious - ly we watch its face,
4. Tic! Tic! Tic! Tic! Brave - ly work, old clock, a - way

Tic! Tic! Tic! Tic! Mark-ing sec-onds one by one, Tic! Tic! Tic! Tic!
Tic! Tic! Tic! Tic! 'Tis the first thing that we hear. Tic! Tic! Tic! Tic!
Tic! Tic! Tic! Tic! Each im - pa-tient in his place. Tic! Tic! Tic! Tic!
Tic! Tic! Tic! Tic! Thro' the night and thro' the day ; Tic! Tic! Tic! Tic!

Car - ing not for rain or sun Tic! Tic! Tic! Tic! Still the clock goes on.
Still it says in ac-cents clear, Tic! Tic! Tic! Tic! As it worketh on.
Till the play hour comes apace. Tic! Tic! Tic! Tic! And the clock goes on.
Wheth-er we may work or play, Tic! Tic! Tic! Tic! Still, old clock, work on.

MODERATO.

1. Some fields there are, that are lost and won, With ne'er a flash of the
2. A field is won when we on-ward pass, Thro' well learn'd tasks to the
3. Nev - er ap-pall'd by a prob-lem, when It has been done it can
4. Our stars are the eyes of those we love, Who watch o'er us as the

boom-ing gun; With ne'er a gleam of the sword in air, But
goal—suc - cess; And this the lev - er of might we ply, The
be a - gain; Now on thro' in - ter - est, tret and tare, And
stars a - bove; Who toil'd like us, and who would not yield, 'Till,

CHORUS.

stars, a ban - ner of stars is there. Hon - or the win - ner, the
stern re-solve, to the tune "I'll try." Hon - or, &c.
knot-ty roots of the cube and square. Hon - or, &c.
step by step they had won the field. Hon - or, &c.

wreath of bay, We twine for him who hath gain'd the day.

Welcome to Teacher. G. F. R. 183

JOYFULLY.

1. Wel-come, thrice wel-come a - gain, our own; Wel-come, thrice wel-come a-
2. Wel-come, thrice wel-come at last to you; Wel-come, thrice wel-come at
3. Wel-come, thrice wel-come to home and heart, War - ble a blithe glad-some

gain: We've won-der'd, and wait - ed and watch'd so long, While
last: We'll meet ev - 'ry task with a cheer - ful glow, For the
lay: We shall look now no more on the va - cant chair, For the

fad - ed the smile - light and hush'd the song, And
smile we have lov'd in the long a - go Is
teach - er we greet fills the old place there, And

wait - ed and watch'd in vain, And wait - ed and watch'd in vain.
nev - er with frowns o'er-cast, Is nev - er with frowns o'er-cast.
this is a hap - py day, And this is a hap - py day.

SANTA CLAUS.

B. R. H.

ALLEGRETTO.

1. Up - on the house, no de -
2. Look in the stock - ings of

lay no pause, Clat - ter the steeds of San - ta Claus;
Lit - tle Will, Ha ! is it not a "glo - rious bill?"

Down thro' the chim-ney with loads of toys, Ho for the lit - tle ones,
Ham - mer and gim - let and lots of tacks, Whis tle and whirl - i - gig,

CHORUS.

Christ mas joys. O! O! O! Who would-n't go, O! O! O!
whip that cracks. O! O! O! &c.

Who would-n't go, Up - on the house - top, click! click! click!

Down thro' the chimney with good St Nick.

3. Snow-white stocking of little Nell,
Oh pretty Santa cram it well ;
Leave her a dolly that laughs and cries,
One that can open and shut its eyes,

4. Here are the stockings of Lazy Jim,
What will the good Saint do for him ?
Lo! he is filling them up with bran
There, he is adding a new ratan !

5. Pa, ma, and Uncle, and Grandma too,
All I declare have something new ;
Even the baby enjoys his part,
Shaking a rattle, now bless his heart.

6. Rover come here, are you all alone,
Haven't they tossed you an extra bone ?
Here's one to gladden your honest jaws
Now wag a "thank'ee" to Santa Claus.

Now we say Farewell.—ROUND, IN TWO PARTS.

Now we say fare - well, Our pleas - ant work is done: Good

bye then, good bye then all Un - til to - mor-row's sun.

Rippling Fast, Rippling Still. G. F. R.

MODERATO.

La, la, la, la, la, la, la, la, la, la, la, la, la, la, la, la;

1. Rip-pling fast, rip-pling still, Whith-er go - est thou, O rill? I
2. Rip-pling fast, rip-pling still, O, what find - est thou, sweet rill? I
3. Rip-pling fast, rip-pling still, Say where hast thou been, O rill? In

go where birds and flow-ers dwell; They know me and they love me well:
find with - in an o - pen glade A griev-ing, weep-ing lit - tle maid,
sad days gone I wan-der'd far, Where ebb'd and flow'd the tide of war,

The Red Bird comes in noon-tide heat, To bathe his cun - ning feet;
Lost in the glen. Home! home! the song I sing, and spar - kle on;
And wept to find my bird - ies flown, And all the flow - ers gone;

Then perch - ing   on   the   near - est   twig,   To   dry   his   coat   and
Home with the gush - ing,   gur-gling   rill,   She   finds   the   cot - tage
I   hushed my   song,   and   soft - ly   crept   Just where   a   wound - ed

fix   his   wig,   He   pours from   out   his   swell - ing   throat   His
by   the   hill, While   on   I   seek   the   for - est   dim,   Still
sol - dier slept;   I   whis-per'd low,   he   woke   to   life,   To

dear   and   mel - low note.   La,   la,   la,   la,   la,   la,   la,   la,   la,   la,
sing - ing   low   my   hymn.   La,   la,   &c.
chil - dren, home and wife.   La,   la,   &c.

la,   la,   la,   la,   la,   la,   la,   la,   la,   la,   la,   la,   la,   la,   la,   la, la, la, la, la, la, la, la, la, la, la, la, la, la, la, la, la,

la, la, la, la, la, la, la, la, la, la, la, la, la, la, la, la.

Learning the Lesson.

D.R.H.

ALLEGRETTO.

1. "I'm learn-ing my les - son," said Ned - die to Kate, "For I
2. "It's just so,"said Kate,"with the patch-work I hate, I am
3. "But how would it be, Kate, with you and with me, If both

al - ways can play so much bet - ter, When tasks are well done, and I'm
sew-ing now o - ver and o - ver; Then grand-ma has said, that my
left to our own way-ward ac-tions? I'd like as a man to know

off for a run, With my les - sons all learn'd to the let - ter:
books may be read, (I will read them from cov - er to cov - er:)
more if I can, (I have now on - ly ci-pher'd thro' Frac-tions:)

I feel like a boy who has much to en - joy, With the
This earth, as I look, seems a ver - y grand book— I do
For ig - nor - ant men, in nine ca - ses in ten, Are 'most

bees, and the birds and the flow-ers; If work is not done, there's small
wish I could read it all, Ned-die; If on - ly the world a whit
sure to be thieves and gar-rot - ers; And, Kate, sure-ly you should learn

pros-pect of fun, For the sport is not hon - est - ly ours.
fast - er was whirl'd, We would be man and wo - man al - rea - dy.
some-thing more, too, If the wo - men are bound to be vot - ers.

Crowding Awfully.

H. R. R.

Published in sheet form with symphony and accompaniment for the piano, by Root & Cady. Price 35 cts

* 1. These Temp'rance folks do crowd us aw - ful - ly, Crowd us
I'm not the man to lose my lib - er - ty, Lose my
2. They stick the pledge these blue tee - to - tal - ers, Blue tee
They talk of woe and want and pov - er - ty, Want and
3. I wish these chaps would cease to pi - ty me, Cease to
Though come to search my once fat pock - et book Once fat

aw - ful - ly, Crowd us aw - ful - ly, Temp'rance folks do
lib - er - ty, Lose my lib - er - ty, Not the man to
to - tal - ers, Blue tee - to - tal - ers, Stick the pledge, these
pov - er - ty, Want and pov - er - ty, Talk of woe and
pi - ty me, Cease to pi - ty me, Wish these chaps would
pock - et book Once fat pock - et book Come to search my

crowd us aw - ful - ly You need - n't think I care. }
lose my lib - er - ty I ha'nt a bit to spare. } I'd
blue tee - to - tal - ers Be - neath each ru - by nose. }
want and pov - er - ty There's truth in that I s'pose. } My
cease to pi - ty me I'm not yet quite be - reft. }
once fat pock - et book There's na - ry six - pence left. } There's a

like to know what's all this fuss a - bout, Is some-thing smash-ing
coat I know is ra - ther see - dy And my pants are tat - ter'd
wife down town would smile like Ve - nus If I'd sign the pledge this

through? They hold their meet - ings round e - ter - nal - ly I
too. My right foot goes but poor - ly boot - ed And the
day. There's a bright hair'd child would jump and ca - per, You may

CHORUS.

won - der what they'll do! Then for - ward boys hur - rah! We'll
left one wears a shoe! Then for - ward &c.
pass the pledge this way! Then for - ward &c.

join the glo - rious fray, We'll hoist our flag and

on to vic - to - ry, The Right shall gain the day.*

* This song may be sung in character to great advantage either by a boy or an adult, pointing in turn to his boot, his shoe, producing his "once fat bocket-book" &c. The chorus whether a quartetto or a larger number should sit on the stage just behind him. One of their number should have a paper representing the Pledge All should remain seated while singing the chorus, until the last one, when the solo singer on reaching the line "you may pass"&c, should turn round, take the pledge from the one who is holding it, and leading off on the chorus should advance to the front of the stage waving it above his head. The last chorus should be sung standing, all rising quickly and singing with great spirit.

13

Sweet Spring-time.—Solo and Chorus.   n. w. j.

SOLO. ALLEGRETTO

1. Come to our bow'rs a - gain, come with your song,   Black-bird and Red-breast,
2. Buds that are sleep-ing in or - chard and bower,   Spring to new life in the
3. Come, build your nest by my cot - tage door,   War-ble your twi-light

lin - ger not long; O, lin - ger not long in that far off clime; We will
soft A - pril shower; With song and the bloom of a sun - nier clime, O,
hymns once more; And pour your glad notes in the morn - ing chime, And

SOLO OR SEMI-CHORUS.

wel - come you back in the sweet spring time. Wel - come,
has - ten thee back in the sweet spring time.
glad - den our hearts in the sweet spring time.

CHORUS.

In the spring time,

wel - come, wel-come wel-come back in the sweet spring time.

in the spring time wel-come, wel-come back in the sweet spring time.

Morning Call.

MODERATO

1. O, haste, broth-ers, haste the sun-shine is clear! No
2. Come, all, broth-ers, all, nor lon-ger de-lay; The

morning hours waste in in-do-lence here: We'll shout and we'll sing, till
wildwoods clear call is, up and a-way; We'll brush off the dew from

morn-ing is done; The wildwood shall ring with our frol-ic and fun.
mead-ows and glen, Nor rest till, a-new, eve re-stores it a-gain.

194   **Follow Your Leader.** (TEMPERANCE.)   B. R. H.

MARCHING SONG.

1. Hark! how your lead - er's bu - gle is sound - ing,
2. Hark! how your lead - er's bu - gle is sound - ing
3. Hark! how your lead - er's bu - gle is sound - ing,

D. C. Hark! how your lead - er's bu - gle is sound - ing,
D. C. Hark! how your lead - er's bu - gle is sound - ing,
D. C. Hark! how your lead - er's bu - gle is sound - ing,

Up! up! my boys, we must meet the foe; Hear ye his cry as a-
Up with the en - sign and charge the foe; Heed we his cry as u-
Quick take the step, on we go, we go; Ech - o his shout as a-

Up! up! my boys, we must meet the foe; Hear ye his cry as a-
Up with the en - sign and charge the foe; Hear we his cry as a-
Quick take the step, on we go, we go; Ech - o his shout as a-

FINE.

way he is bound-ing, Ho! fol low me, ho! fol-low me, ho! fol-low me, ho!
way he is bound-ing, Ho! fol-low me, ho! fol-low me, ho! fol-low me, ho!
way he is bound-ing, Ho! fol-low me, ho! fol-low me, ho! fol-low me, ho!

way he is bound-ing, Ho! fol-low me, ho! fol-low me, ho! fol-low me, ho!
way he is bound-ing, Ho! fol-low me, ho! fol-low me, ho! fol-low me, ho!
way he is bound-ing, Ho! fol-low me, ho! fol-low me, ho! fol-low me, ho!

Quick, dou - ble quick is the word and the mo - tion,
Tem-p'rance we bring, for the wound - ed a heal - er,
Hail! ye whose hearth-stones are shroud - ed with sor - row,

In - to the ranks or re - tire to the rear,
Hope for the hope - less and comfort for dis - may,
Look through your tears to the dawning of the day,

No - ble the cause, let us prove our de - vo - tion,
Help for the drunk - ard and law for the deal - er,
Err - ing ones join us, nor wait for the mor - row,

D. C.

Nev - er a faint heart, nev - er a fear, No, no, no.
On to the front, boys, in - to the fray, Yes, yes, yes.
Fly from the tempt - er, haste ye a - way, Yes, yes, yes.

SWEET BIRD

G. F. R.

CHEERFULLY.

1. Come to the meadows a - gain, sweet bird,
2. Come to the meadows a - gain, sweet bird,
3. Come to the meadows a - gain, sweet bird,
4. Come to the meadows a - gain, sweet bird,

Come to the meadows a - gain; We've waited and lis - tened so
Come to the meadows a - gain; The cow - slips are open - ing their
Come to the meadows a - gain; The lit - tle blue bells of the
Come to the meadows a - gain; The zeph-yrs are breath-ing their

wea - ry and long, The sound of your pip - ing, the
bright star - ry eyes; The dai - sies and but - ter - cups
vi - o - lets peep From un - der the moss - es where
o - dors of balm, From sweet south - ern lands where the

joy of your song And the trill of your mu - si - cal strain.
soon will a - rise, With their bril - liant and blos - som - ing train,
they've been a - sleep, And all smi - - ling they wel - come the rain.
or - ange and palm Wave their plu - mage of beau - ti - ful green.

CHORUS.

Come, come a - gain, sweet bird. Come, come a -

Come to the meadows a - gain, sweet bird, Come to the meadows a -

gain, sweet bird, Sweet...... bird. Sweet......

gain, sweet bird. Come a - gain,

bird.

Come a - gain; Come to the mead - ows a - gain.

"Millions of Tiny Rain Drops."

G. F. R.

From the "Coronet."

INSTRUMENT. *Play the accompaniment an octave higher than it is written.*

ALLEGRETTO.

1. Mil - lions of ti - ny rain - drops Are fall - ing all a - round;
2. A light and air - y tre - ble They play up - on the stream;
3. Oh! 'tis a storm of mu - sic, And Rob - ins don't in - trude,

They're danc - ing on the house - tops, They're hid - ing in the ground:
And the mel - o - dy en - chants us, Like the mu - sic of a dream:
If, when the rain is wea - ry, They sing an in - ter - lude:

They are fair - y - like mu - si - cians, With a - ny - thing for keys,
A deep - er base is sound - ing When they're drop - ping in - to caves,
It seems as if the war - bling Of the birds in all the bow'rs,

Beating tunes up - on the   win - dows, Keeping time up - on the   trees;
With a ten - or from the   zeph - yrs, And an al - to from the   waves;
Had gath - er'd in the   rain - drops, And was com - ing down in   show'rs;

They are fair - y - like mu - si - cians, With a - ny - thing for   keys,
A deep - er base is   sound - ing, When they're drop-ping in - to   caves,
It seems as if the   war - bling Of birds in all the   bow'rs,

Beating tunes up - on the   win - dows, Keeping time up - on the   trees.
With a ten - or from the   zeph - yrs, And an al - to from the   waves.
Had been gath - er'd in - to   rain - drops, And was com - ing down in   show'rs.

The Farmer's Song. B. R. R.

Milk Maid's Song
for 1st and 2d ver. Hap - py mor - tals, to your
Milk Maid's Song Wear - y mor - tals, cease your
for 3d verse.
MODERATO.

1. Up the steeps the morn is bound - ing, Hark! the milk maid's
2. Now while earth and sky are glow - ing, Speed the plow - ing,
3. Now the west - ern sun de - scend - ing, Shad - ows with the

por - tals comes the day, the
la - bor, comes the close of

song is sound - ing, Voice of bird and bee re - sound - ing;
speed the mow - ing, Gay the song that cheers our go - ing;
light are blend - ing; Lo! the herds are home - ward wend - ing;

gold - en day.
gold - en day.

Up, my lads, be blithe as they, A - way, a - way, a - way.
Glad - ly toil we while we may, A - way, a - way, a - way.
Cease the toil, but not the lay, A - way, a - way, a - way.

CHORUS.
ALLEGRETTO.

Cheer - i - ly, cheer - i - ly we heed the call, heed the call,
Mer - ri - ly, mer - ri - ly we hast - en all, hast - en all,

heed the call; Cheer - i - ly, cheer - i - ly we heed the call,
hast - en all; Mer - ri - ly, mer - ri - ly we hast - en all,

FINE.   SECOND TIME pp

To 1st and 2d release Hail to the dawn of day.   Oh sing with the maid and the
To 3d cluster Sing with the close of day.   Oh sing, &c.
To 1st and 3d D.C. Forth with a hap - py lay.
To 3d D. C. Home with a hap - py lay.

bird and the hum - ble - bee. La, la, la, la, la, La,

la, la, la, la, la, la, Sweet - ly we join in the

The Farmer's Song.—Concluded.

After Repeat D. C. to Chorus.

glad - some mel - o - dy, La, la, la, la, la, la, la,

ALLEGRETTO.   **The New Dress.**   B. R. H.

1. I missed dear lit - tle Ma - bel from her class and school one
2. Well if sweet lit - tle Ma - bel's moth - er is so ver - y
3. "I will," cried man - y lit - tle ones "and I," cried man - y
4. The plan at once de - cid - ed, then to stud - y as be -

day, And asked the oth - er chil --dren "was she
poor, How ma - ny of these chil - dren now will
more, "We'll soft - ly go some eve - ning dark and
fore, The dress was quick - ly pur-chased and was

sick or gone a - way, "When a wee one blushed and
give a dime or more, To buy an - oth - er
hang it on her door, She will nev - er know who
hung on Ma - bel's door, And eve - ry eye was

stam - mered, " nei - ther sick nor an - y where,
school dress so that Ma - bel shall not stay,
hung it but will rath - er think I guess
bright with joy, and ev - ery heart was gay,

.On - ly her Moth - er keeps her home, she
Need - ing the prop - er clo - thing from her
God in His pi - ty for His child has
When lit - tle Ma - bel smil - ing came in

has no dress to wear," On - ly her Moth - er
school an - oth - er day? Need - ing the prop - er
given her this new dress." God in His pit - y
her new dress next day. When lit - tle Ma - bel

keeps her home, she has no dress to wear.
cloth - ing from her school an - oth - er day.
for his child, has given her this new dress.
smil - ing came, in her new dress next day:

Ah! how, Sophia.

Arr. for this work.

FIRST DIVISION.

Ah! how, So - phi - a, can you leave, can you

leave Your lov - er, your lov - er, and of hope be - reave!

SECOND DIVISION.

Go fetch the Indian's bor-row'd plume, bor - row'd plume; Yet

rich - er, yet rich - er far than that your bloom:

THIRD DIVISION.

I'm but a lodg - er in her heart, in her heart; And

more than me, and more than me I fear have

FIRST DIVISION.

Ah! how, So - phia, Ah! how, So-

SECOND DIVISION.

Go, go, go, go fetch the Indian's, fetch the

THIRD DIVISION.

part,

phia,   Ah! how, So-phia, Ah! how, So-phia, phia,

Indian's, fetch the Indian's, fetch the Indian's,   Go fetch the

I'm   but   a   lodg - er,   I'm   but   a

phia, Ah! how, So - phia, phia,   phia, Ah! how, So - phia, phia,

Indian's,   Go   fetch the Indian's,   Go fetch the

lodg - er,   I'm but a lodg - er,   I'm   but a

phia, Ah! how, So-phia, phia,   phia, Ah! how, So - phia. Ah! how, So-

Indian's,   Go fetch the Indian's, fetch the Indian's, fetch the

lodg - er,   I'm but a lodg - er, _ _   _ _   I'm   but a

phi - a, can you leave, Ah! how, So - phia, phia,

In - dian's bor - row'd plume, Go fetch the

lodg - er in her heart, I'm but a

phia, Ah! how, So - phia, phia, phia, Ah! how, So - phia, Ah! how. So-

Indian's Go fetch the In-dian's, fetch the Indian's, fetch the

lodg - er, I'm but a lodg - er, I'm but a

phi - a, can you leave, Ah! how, So-phia, Ah! how, So-phia.

Indian's bor-row'd plume; Ah! how, So-phia, phia, phia, Ah! how, So-phia.

lodg - er iu her heart; Ah! how, So-phia, phia, phia. Ah! how, So-phia.

When the Old Year Died.

R. R. R. 207

1. There were ring - ing notes in the fes - tal throng,
2. There were strick - en forms at the lone - ly hearth
3. And a prayer a - rose in that home of doom
4. And the New Year came with a song of mirth

With the dan - cers feet, and the swell of song,
When the news was told to the wait - ing earth,
O'er the child of time at his o - pen tomb,
As the smile of Spring to the wea - ry earth,

There were forms of beau - ty, and forms of pride,
And a tear a - lone to the notes re - plied,
And the wait - ing ser - aph heaven - ward hied
As a grate - ful token to the heart un - tried,

When the deep chime fell, and the Old Year died.
When the deep chime fell, and the Old Year died.
As the deep chime fell, and the Old Year died.
When the deep chime fell, and the Old Year died.

14

BEAUTIFUL ANGEL

G. F. R.

1. Beau - ti - ful An - gel on pin - ions of light, Wait till I whis - per my Moth - er good night;
2. Beau - ti - ful An - gel, her sor - row is sore, Weep-ing for one who will weep nev - er - more;
3. Beau - ti - ful An - gel, thrice bless - ed art thou! See, there's a smile on the dear pal - lid brow;

List while she calls me her pride and her joy, Folds to her bo - som her
Waft her sweet dreams of the bless-ed a - bove, Tell her, our God is a
To - ken of faith that hath conquered her fears, To-ken that time will have

own lit - tle boy, Hov - er a - round her on pin - ions of light,
Fa - ther of love; On - ly for this, am I stay - ing my flight,
so - lace for tears: Prest to those lips in their ag - o - ny white,

Moth - er, dear Moth - er, O! kiss me good night.
Moth - er, dear Moth - er, O! kiss me good night.
Moth - er, dear Moth - er, for - ev - er good night,

Will you Sing after Us?

G. F. R,

MODERATO

1. Will you sing af - ter us? O, yes. Just what we sing? *Just*
2. Will you sing af - ter us? O, yes. Just what we sing? *Just*

what you sing; Well, Do, re, mi; *Do, re, mi;* Do, re, mi, fa, sol;
what you sing; Well, Ha, ha, ha, *Ha, ha, ha;* Ha, ha, ha, ha, ha;

Do, re, mi, fa, sol; Do, re, mi, fa, sol, la, si, *Do, re, mi, fa, sol, la, si,*
Ha, ha, ha, ha, ha; Ha, ha, ha, ha, ha, ha, ha, *Ha, ha, ha, ha, ha, ha, ha,*

Do, re, mi, fa, sol, la, si, do, re, do, si, la, sol, fa, mi, re, *Do, re, mi, fa,*
Ha, ha, ha, ha, ha, ha, ha, ha, ha, ha, ha, ha, ha, ha, ha, *Ha, ha, ha, ha,*

sol, la, si, do, re, do, si, la, sol, la, mi, re, do. That's right, that's right.
ha, ha, ha, ha, ha, ha, ha, ha, ha, ha, ha, ha, ha. That's right, that's right.

Divide the class into two divisions, one to sing the words in Roman letters, the other those in *Italics*.

Morning Song. B. R. H.

NOTE.—It is likely that in most schools but one part will generally be sung, but a piece like the following depends for its full effect, so much upon the blending of all the parts that it is hoped the teacher will contrive to have them all represented. Let those who sing the sustained notes do so with the swelling tone.

1. The morn - ing is beam - ing, the morn - ing is beam - ing
2. The hill - tops are glow - ing, the hill - tops are glow - ing,
3. The brook - lets are dash - ing, the brook - lets are dash - ing,

The morn - ing is beam - ing,
The hill - tops are glow - ing,
The brook - lets are dash - ing,

Oh, has - ten the sight to be - hold, The
With light like a man - tle of snow, The
O'er peb - bles of crim - son and white, The

Oh, hast - en the sight to be-hold, The
With light like a man - tle of snow, The
O'er peb - bles of crim-son and white, The

moun - tains are gleam - ing, the moun - tains are gleam - ing, With
cat - tle are low - ing, the cat - tle are low - ing, As
riv - ers are flash - ing, the riv - ers are flash - ing, Their

moun - tains are gleam - ing With
cat - tle are low - ing, As
riv - ers are flash - ing, Their

tint - ings of pur - ple and gold; The
forth to the mead - ows they go; Their
ar - rows of sil - ver - y light; Thus

tint - ings of pur-ple and gold.
forth to the mead-ows they go.
ar - rows of sil - ver - y light.

for - ests are ring - ing with bright birds sing - ing, To
mel - low bells' jin - gle makes glad - some tin - gle, To
mead - ow and moun - tain and grove and foun - tain, Re

wel-come the com - ing of day. Up! slum-ber - ing mor-tals and
wel-come the com - ing of day. Up! &c.
joice at the com - ing of day. Up! &c.

bring from your port-als A greet-ing as glad as they, Hil - lil -

Morning Song.—CONCLUDED.

li - lo, Hil - lil - li - lo, We hail the dawn of the morn-ing

Hil-lil - li - lo, li - lo, li - lo,

Hil - lil - li - lo. Hil - lil - li - lo, We wel-come the com-ing day.

Make Hay while the Sun Shines.

B. R. H.

MODERATO

1. Make hay, while the sun shines, When the day is bright and calm ;'Till the
2. Make hay, while the sun shines, As the bees lay up their store ; For the
3. Make hay, while the sun shines, Gather in life's precious store ; Ere the
4. Make hay, while the sun shines,'Till the toil of life is done ; And a

1st time. 2d time.

welcome rest shall sooth thy breast, In the evening's hour of balm. balm.
win-try blast will come at last, And the bright flowers bloom no more. more.
gold - en morn of youth is gone, And the bright days come no more. more.
calm sweet rest shall sooth thy breast, When the work of life is won. won.

Farewell to Teacher.

MODERATO.

1. Fare-well! If not on earth we meet, We will not grieve to
For they, whose life - work is com-plete, Shall dwell in bliss for-
2. Fare-well! The paths that now di - verge May ne'er be re - u-
And tho'ts sweep o'er us, surge on surge Of bless - ings un - re-

sev - er; }
ev - er: } Thy glance was on a bright - er shore, While
ni - ted; }
qui - ted: } May He, who keeps thee in his care, With

steps of sci - ence tra - cing; The earth - ly and the
love di - vine and ten - der; In an - swer to our

heav'n - ly lore, In beau - ty in - ter - la - cing.
grate - ful pray'r, Those bless - ings doub - ly ren - der.

Rallying Song for Bands of Hope. G. F. R.

MODERATO.

1. Lo, the ranks of youth and beau - ty,
Hope, her cheer - ing song sings o'er them,
2. Ral - ly, boys and girls, we need you,
Rum is strong, but truth is strong - er,
3. Speeds the glo - rious re - form - a - tion,
Rum shall cease its reign of ter - ror,

At the call of truth and du - ty, March a-
Vic - t'ry is the prize be - fore them, Far a-
Ral - ly! join some band and speed you, Speed a-
Rum must rule the earth no long - er; Then a-
Speeds the hour when from the na - tion Swept a-
And be - fore the truth, the er - ror Shrink a-

| 1ST TIME. | 2D TIME.

way, a - way, a - way, a - way;
way, a - way, a-.................way, a - way.
way, a - way, a - way, a - way;
way, a - way, a-.................way, a - way.
way, a - way, a - way, a - way;
way, a - way, a-.................way, a - way.

CHORUS.

The bands of hope are march-ing A - way, a - way, The

bands of hope are march-ing on, And vic-t'ry must and shall be won,

A - way, a - way; The bands of hope are march - ing,

A - way, a - way, The bands of hope are march - ing.

The Beacon Light.

G. F. R.

ANDANTINO.

1. We are sail - ing o'er an
2. Though the skies are dark a -
3. He will keep it ev - er

o - cean, To a far and for - eign shore; And the
bove us, And the waves are dash - ing high, Let us
burn - ing, From the light - house of His love; And it

waves are dash - ing 'round us, And we hear the break - ers
look to - ward the bea - con, We shall reach it by and
al - ways shines the bright - est When the skies are dark a -

roar: But we look a - bove the bil - lows, In the
by: 'Tis the light of God's great mer - cy, And He
bove: If we keep our eyes up - on it, And we

dark - ness   of   the   night; And   we   see   the   stead - y
holds   it   up   in   view,   As   a   guide - star   to - his
steer   our   course   a - right,   We   shall   reach   the   har - bor

CHORUS.

gleam - ing   Of   our   change - less   bea - con   light.   O,   the
chil - dren,   As   a   guide   to   me   and   you.   O,   &c.
safe - ly,   By   the   bless - ed   bea - con   light.   O,   &c.

light   is   flash - ing   bright - ly,   From   a   calm   and   storm - less   shore,

Where   we   hope   to   cast   our   an - chor,   When   our   voy - ag - ing   is   o'er.

Words by Dr. Blackall,   # The Union Greeting.   G. C. P.

1. Hith-er we come, as a Un-ion Band, To sing sweet songs of a
2. Greet-ing we give on this fes-tive night, A hap-py lay of the

bet-ter land, The land of peace and love; Where Je-sus reigns as a
heart's de-light, Good will on ev-ery hand; Bright eyes are beam-ing a-

King a-lone, And all His chil-dren fond-ly own Their
mid the throng, And young hearts glow as they sing the song Of

CHORUS.

Fa-ther, God a-bove. Oh! mer-ri-ly, mer-ri-ly,
this our Un-ion Band. Oh! &c.

joy - ous and free, Sing we the song cf the true;

Cheer - i - ly, cheer - i - ly, hap - py are we, Warm is our wel-come to

BOYS. GIRLS. TOGETHER.

you. Wel - come! wel - come! Warm is our wel-come to you!

3. Gems have we brought to delight the soul,
   And flowers whose fragrance shall o'er be whole,
       That cheer life's way along;
   Then give your hearts and extend your hands,
   And let us bind you in silken bands,
       The bands of love and song.

CHORUS—Oh! joyously, joyously sound we the strain,
           For 'tis the song of the true;
       Cheerily, cheerily give we again,
           Welcome, thrice welcome to you.
               Welcome! welcome!
       Welcome, thrice welcome to you.

The Valley of Chamouni.

From Glover.
Arr. by F. W. R.

SOLO. ALLEGRETTO

1. When the heart in gold-en fan-cies, To the sway of happiest dreams, Back to
2. When I hear the Alp-horn ring-ing, When Mount Blanc fore-tells the day, And the

CHORUS

1. When the heart in gold-en fan-cies, To the sway of hap-piest dreams, Then back to
2. When I hear the Alp-horn ring-ing, When Mount Blanc foretells the day, And when the

scenes of beau-ty glan-ces, Lit by mem - 'ry's brightest beams; Then I
breeze of morn-ing bring-ing, Moun-tain chime and mountain lay ; Then once

scenes of beau-ty glan-ces, Lit by mem-'ry's bright-est beams; 'Tis then I
breeze of morn-ing bring-ing, Moun-tain chime and moun-tain lay ; O, then once

see that vale of foun-tains, Where the Alpflow'rs woo the gale; Un-der
more with rap ture glow-ing, All that moun-tain land I hail; But my

see that vale of fountains, Where the Alp-flow'rs woo the gale; Yes un-der
more with rap-ture glow-ing, All that moun-tain-land I hail; But still my

all   the snow-crown'd mountains Shin-ing o'er   that beau-teous vale;   Oh!
heart   with joy o'er - flow - ing, Lin-gers in   that beau-teous vale;   Oh!

all the snow-crown'd mountains,Shin-ing o'er that beau-teous vale; Oh!
heart with joy o'er - flow-ing, Lin-gers in that beau-teous vale; Oh!

Cha-mou-ni, sweet Cha-mou-ni, Oh! the vale of Cha-mou-ni!   Oh!
Cha-mou-ni, sweet Cha-mou-ni, Oh! the vale of Cha-mou-ni!   Oh!

Cha-mou-ni, sweet Cha-mou-ni; Oh! vale of Cha-mou-ni,sweet vale; Oh!
Cha-mou-ni, sweet Cha-mou-ni; Oh! vale of Cha-mou-ni,sweet vale; Oh!

Cha-mou-ni, sweet Cha-mou-ni, Oh! Cha-mou-ni's sweet vale.
Cha-mou-ni, sweet Cha-mou-ni Oh! Cha-mou-ni's sweet vale.

Cha-mou-ni, sweet Cha-mou-ni, Oh! Cha-mou-ni's sweet vale,sweet vale.
Cha-mou-ni, sweet Cha-mou-ni, Oh! Cha-mou-ni's sweet vale,sweet vale.

On the Mountain High.—Solo and Chorus. G. F. R.

SOLO, OR SEMICHORUS. From "Festival Glee Book," by permission.
ALLEGRETTO.

1. On the moun-tain high he's roam-ing, In the bright and glo-rious
2. When the shades of eve are fall-ing, And the mel-low horn is

CHORUS.

La, la, la, la, la, la, la, la, la, la, la, la, la, la, la, la, la, la,

morn-ing, To the cham-ois fleet give warn-ing, For my
call-ing, Then my hunt-er, home re-turn-ing, Glad-ly

la, la, la, la, la, la, la, la, la, la, la, la, la, la, la, la, la, la,

hunt-er's brave and true. La, la, la, la, la, la,
joins our mer-ry lay. La, la, &c.

la, la, la, la, la, la, la, la, la, la, la, la, la,

la, la, la, la, la, la, la, la, la, la, la,
la, la,
la, la, la, la, la, la, la, la, la, la, la, la, la, la,
la, la,

la, la, la, la, la, la, la, la, la, la,
la, la, la, la, la, la, la, la, la, la, la,
la, la, la, la,

la. On the moun-tain high he's
la,
la, la, la, la, la, la. On the moun-tain high he's roam-ing, La, la,
la,
15

On the Mountain High.—Concluded.

roam - ing,   Iu   the   bright   and   glo   -   rious

la, la. la, la, la;   In   the   bright and   glo - rious morn - ing,   La,   la,

morn - ing,   To   the   cham   -   ois   fleet   give

la, la, la, la, la,   To   the   cham-ois   fleet   give   warn - ing,   La,   la,

warn - ing,   For   my   hunt - er's   brave   and   true.

la, la, la, la, la,   For   my   hunt - er's   brave and   true,   brave and   true.

SONGS, HYMNS, ANTHEMS AND CHANTS,

FOR WORSHIP.

We Praise Thee, O, our Father.

G. F. R.

MODERATO.

1. For all the beau-teous birds that sing, In field, and bush and tree,
2. For all the bright and fra-grant flow'rs Of mead-ow, wood and glade,
3. For clear blue skies that smile se - rene O'er deep blue waves be - low;
4. And may these fair and love - ly things, That Thy dear hand hath giv'n,

And make the air, at dawn - ing, ring, With won-d'rous mel - o - o - dy,
The love-liest of all gifts of ours, That Thou for us hath made,
For ear - ly morn-ing's ros - y sheen, And sun-set's crim - son glow,
Lift up, as tho' on an - gels' wings, Our tho'ts to Thee and heav'n.

We praise Thee, O, our Fa - ther, We praise Thee, O, our Fa - ther.

"To Thee, O God and Savior." W. J. Robjohn.

MODERATO.

1. To thee, O God and Sav - ior, our praise and thanks we bring,
2. But for our pres - er - va - tion thro' per - ils of the night,
3. O help us, Lord, we pray thee, a - gainst our foes with - in;

O bend from thy throne, Lord, and hear us while we sing;
For shield - ing our slum - bers from dan - ger by thy might,
Give strength and de - sire, Lord, to fight and con - quer sin;

For mer - cies past and pres - ent, for all we have and are,
We chief - ly now de - sire, Lord, to of - fer up this day
That, day by day as - cend - ing, we may draw near - er thee,

We bless thy name; Lord, hear us, and be not a - far.
Our thank - ful songs, and for pro - tec - tion yet to pray.
Un - til with - in thy king-dom's gates thy face we see.

We Praise Thee. (OPENING OR CLOSING.) 8. F. R. 227

1. We praise Thee—we bless Thee, our Fath - er, and Friend,
2. We thank Thee for bless - ings re - ceived eve - ry day—
3. Pro - tect us— de - fend us from sin and from harm,

O let our de - vo - tions be - fore Thee as - cend;
For which Thou hast taught us un - ceas - ing to pray;
As the shep - herd doth gath - er the lambs with his arm:

In youth and in child - hood, to - geth - er we come,
But O, for the treas - ures Thy Word hath in store,
O nour - ish and strength-en our souls now in youth,

To pray that Thy will in our hearts may be done.
Thy name, O, our Fath - er we bless and a - dore
With Thy love and Thy wis - dom,—Thy good - ness and truth.

Draw Nigh to Us.

MODERATO.

1. Draw nigh to us, our Fath - er, By draw-ing us to thee,
2. We hail Thee throned in glo - ry—'Mid heaven's angelic throng,

And may we here to - geth - er, Thy wondrous glo - ry see,
Who cast their crowns be - fore Thee With ev - er - last - ing song.

The sun it shin-eth ev - er, Though clouds are o'er its light,
Thy good-ness yet re - joi - ces Love's humblest note to hear,

Thy love would cheer us ev - er If sin dimm'd not our sight.
May then our fee-blest voi - ces At - tract Thy gracious ear.

Jesus gentlest Savior.

1. Je - sus, gent - lest Sa - vior; God of might and pow'r.
2. Out be - yond the shin - ing Of the far - thest star;
3. Je - sus, gent - lest Sa - vior; Thou art in us now.

Make Thy ho - ly dwell - ing In us at this hour.
Thou art ev - er stretch - ing, In - fi - nite - ly far—
Fill us full of good - ness, 'Till our hearts o'er flow.

Na - ture can - not hold thee, Heav'n is all too strait
Yet the hearts of chil - dren, Hold what worlds can - not—
Pray the pray'r with - in us, That to heav'n shall rise.

For thine end - less glo - ry, And thy roy - al state.
And the God of won - ders Loves the low - ly spot.
Sing the song that an - gels, Sing a - bove the skies.

ANDANTINO

1. We come in child - hood's joy - ful - ness, We
   We of - fer up, O God! our hearts, In
2. We come not as the might - y come; Not
   But as the pure in heart should bend; Seek
3. To Thee thou Lord of life and light, A -
   We bend the knee we lift the heart, And

come, as chil - dren, free!)
trust - ing love to Thee.) Well may we bend in
as the proud we bow;)
we thine al - tars now.) "For - bid them not," the
mid the an - gel throng,)
swell the ho - ly song.) How blest the chil - dren

sol - emn joy, At thy bright courts a - bove;
Sav - ior said; But let them come to me;
of the Lord Who wait a - round His throne,

RITARD

Well may the grate-ful child re-joice, In such a Fa-ther's love.
Oh Sav - ior dear we hear Thy call, We come, we come to Thee.
How sweet to tread the path that leads To yon - der heavenly home,

Praise. S. M.

MODERATO

1. Now let our voi - ces join, To form a sa - cred song, Ye
2. How straight the path ap-pears, How o - pen and how fair; No
3. But flowers of par - a - dise In rich pro - fu - sion spring, Tho
4. All hon - or to His name, Who marks the shin - ing way, To

pil - grims in Je - ho - vah's ways, With mu - sic pass a - long.
toils to catch un - wa - ry feet, No fierce de - stroy - er there.
Sun of Glo - ry gilds the path, And dear com - pan - ions sing.
Him who leads the wan-derer on, To realms of end - less day.

Doxology. L. M.

G. F. R.

REVERENTIALLY

To God, the Fa - ther, Spir - it, Son, In soul and mind, and be - ing one; Be

glo - ry, praise and ser - vice given, By all on earth, and all in heaven.

Dismission Hymn.

MODERATO

By permission.

1. All to-geth-er, all to-geth-er. Raise, raise the song.
Ere we sev-er, ere we sev-er Friends, school-mates dear.
2. Thus to-geth-er, would we ev-er, Hand join'd in hand,
When life's les-sons and its la-bors, All, all are o'er.

Sweet the grate-ful strains as-cend-ing, From this glad and hap-py
Join this offer-ing to our Fath-er, For his help and pres-ence
Tread the sa-cred paths of du-ty, On-ward to the Bet-ter
May we with Thy ran-som'd mil-lions, Meet Thee on the Gold-en

CHORUS

throng.
here. Thou, thou the Giv-er Of all earth-ly good to men.
Land.
shore. There, oh Thou Giv-er Of all earth-ly good to men,

Oh may we ev-er Mag-ni-fy Thy worth-y name.
Will we for-ev-er Mag-ni-fy Thy worth-y name.

1. The pur-ple dawn is break-ing, The si-lent groves are wak-ing, Their
2. The pur-ple dawn is break-ing. The world its dreams for-sak-ing, To
3. The pur-ple dawn is break-ing, The night her dark plumes shaking, The

breez-y o-dors shak-ing, The day comes roll-ing on; My
joy-ous life a-wak-ing, The day comes roll-ing on; O
trance of slum-ber break-ing, The day comes roll-ing on; O

prayer to heaven as-cend-ing, With love's pure in-cense blend-ing, To
Fa-ther, while I'm pray-ing, Keep all my heart from stray-ing, Thy
Lord, Thy love re-veal-ing, O'er all my spir-it steal-ing, A-

all Thy Wis-dom bend-ing, As the day comes roll-ing on.
ho-ly will o-bey-ing, As the day comes roll-ing on.
wake my pur-est feel-ing, As the day comes roll-ing on.

Swiftly Glide the Hours.

G. F. R.

MODERATO.

1. Swift - ly glide the hours a - way, Speed - ing
2. Toil and rest a - like he shares, Bless - es
3. If to - day our lives have been Soil'd by
4. In the dark - ness and the light, Keep us

from us day by day; Leav - ing ev - er,
both our joys and cares, Makes them all His
thought or deed of sin; Lord, from us the
ev - er in Thy sight; And to Thy dear

as they move, To - kens of our Fa - ther's love.
good - ness prove, Makes them to - kens of His love.
guilt re - move, Fa - ther, par - don in Thy love.
home a - bove, Fa - ther, guide us in Thy love.

Confession.

G. F. R.

REVERENTIALLY.

1. List - en, O, list - en, our Fa - ther all ho - ly!
2. Pit - y me now, for, my Fa - ther, no sor - row
3. For thy for - give - ness, the gift I am seek - ing,

Hum - ble and sor - row - ful, own - ing my sin;
Ev - er can be like the pain that I know;
Noth - ing, O, noth - ing I of - fer to Thee!

Hear me con - fess, in my pen - i - tence low - ly,
When I re - mem - ber that, all through to - mor - row,
Thou, to my sin - ful and sad spir - it speak - ing,

How, in my weak - ness, temp - ta - tion came in.
Miss - ing the light of thy love I may go.
Giv - ing for - give - ness, giv'st all things to me.

4. Keep me, my Father, O, keep me from falling!
   I had not sinned, had I felt Thou wert nigh;
   Speak, when the voice of the tempter is calling,
   So that temptation before Thee may fly.

5. Thoughts of my sin much more humble shall make me,
   For thy forgiveness I'll love Thee the more:
   So keep me humble until Thou shalt take me
   Where sin and sorrow forever are o'er.

HYMN 1.

1. Awake my soul and with the sun,
Thy daily stage of duty run;
Shake off dull sloth, and joyful rise,
To pay thy morning sacrifice.

2. Glory to thee, who safe hast kept,
And hast refreshed me while I slept;
Grant, Lord, when I from death shall
wake,
I may of endless life partake.

3. Lord, I my vows to thee renew;
Scatter my sins as morning dew;
Guard my first springs of thought
and will,
And with thy soul my spirit fill.

4. Direct, control, suggest, this day,
All I design, or do, or say; [might,
That all my powers, with all their
In thy soul glory may unite.

HYMN 2.

1. Come, O my soul! in sacred lays,
Attempt thy great creator's praise;
But, oh, what tongue can speak his
fame! [theme!
What mortal verse can reach the

2. Enthroned amid the radiant spheres
He glory, like a garment wears;
To form a robe of light divine,
Ten thousand suns around him
shine.

3. In all our Maker's grand designs,
Almighty power, with wisdom
shines: [frame,
His works, thro' all this wondrous
Declare the glory of his name.

4. Raised on devotion's lofty wing,
Do thou, my soul, his glories sing;
And let his praise employ thy tongue
Till listening worlds shall join the
song!

HYMN 3.

1. From all that dwell below the skies,
Let the Creator's praise arise:
Let the redeemer's name be sung,
Thro' ev'ry land—by ev'ry tongue.

2. Eternal are thy mercies Lord;
Eternal truth attends thy word;
Thy praise shall sound from shore
to shore,
Till suns shall rise and set no more,

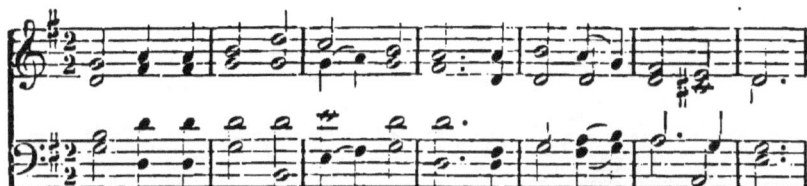

HYMN 4.

1. Lift up to God the voice of praise,
   Whose breath our souls inspired;
   Loud, and more loud, the anthems raise,
   With grateful ardor fired.

2. Lift up to God the voice of praise,
   Whose goodness, passing thought,
   Loads every moment as it flies,
   With benefits unsought.

3. Lift up to God the voice of praise,
   For hope's transporting ray,
   Which lights through darkest age of death.
   To realms of endless day.

HYMN 5.

1. O, that the Lord would guide my ways
   To keep his statutes still!
   O, that my God would grant me grace
   To know and do his will!

2. O, send thy spirit down, to write
   Thy law upon my heart;
   Nor let my tongue indulge deceit,
   Nor act the liar's part.

3. Order my footsteps by thy word,
   And make my heart sincere;
   Let sin have no dominion, Lord,
   But keep my conscience clear.

4. Make me to walk in thy commands,
   'Tis a delightful road;
   Nor let my head, nor heart, nor hands,
   Offend against my God.

HYMN 6.

1. Eternal Source of life and light,
   Supremely good and wise,
   To thee we bring our grateful vows;
   Accept our sacrifice.

2. Our dark and erring mind illume
   With truth's celestial rays;
   Inspire our hearts with heavenly love,
   And tune our lips to praise.

3. Safely conduct us by thy truth,
   Through life's perplexing road;
   And bring us, when our journey's o'er,
   Lord, to thine own abode.

Sicily.

HYMN 7.

1. God is love his mercy brightens
   All the path in which we rove;
   Bliss he wakes, and woe he lightens;
   God is wisdom, God is love.

2. E'en the hour that darkest seemeth
   Will his changeless goodness prove;
   From the gloom his brightness
      streameth:
   God is wisdom, God is love.

3. He with earthly cares entwineth
   Hope and comfort from above:
   Ev'ry where his glory shineth;
   God is wisdom, God is love.

HYMN 8.

1. Heavenly Father! grant thy blessing
   On the teaching of this day;
   That our hearts, thy fear possessing,
   May from sin be turned away.

2. Have we wandered? O, forgive us!
   Have we wished from truth to rove?
   Turn, O, turn us, and receive us,
   And incline our hearts to love.

HYMN 9.

1. When the joyous day is dawning,
   And the happy light we see,
   We, who live in life's pure morning
   Father, would remember thee.

2. While in quiet we were sleeping,
   Kindly, though we knew it not,
   Thou a guardian watch wert keeping,
   Never is thy child forgot.

HYMN 10.

1. Praise to thee, thou great Creator!
   Praise to thee from every tongue;
   Join my soul with every creature,
   Join the universal song.

2. Father, Source of all compassion,
   Pure, unbounded grace is thine;
   Hail the God of our salvation!
   Praise him for his love divine.

3. For ten thousand blessings given,
   For the hope of future joy,
   Sound his praise through earth and
      heaven,
   Sound Jehovah's praise on high.

HYMN 11.

1. God bless our native land,
   May Heaven's protecting hand
   Still guard our shore.
   May Peace her power extend,
   Foe be transformed to friend,
   And all our rights depend
   On war no more.

2. May just and righteous laws
   Uphold the public cause,
   And bless our name;
   Home of the brave and free,
   Stronghold of Liberty—
   We pray that still on thee
   There be no stain.

3. And not this land alone,
   But be thy mercies known
   From shore to shore;
   Lord make the nations see
   That men should brothers be,
   And form one family,
   The wide world o'er

HYMN 12.

1. My country, 'tis of thee,
   Sweet land of liberty,
   Of thee I sing;
   Land where my fathers died,
   Land of the pilgrim's pride;
   From ev'ry mountain side
   Let Freedom ring.

2. My native country! thee,
   Land of the noble free,
   Thy name I love;
   I love thy rocks and rills,
   Thy woods and templed hills;
   My heart with rapture thrills,
   Like that above.

3. Let music swell the breeze,
   And ring from all the trees
   Sweet Freedom's song;
   Let mortal tongues awake;
   Let all that breathe partake:
   Let rocks their silence break,
   The sound prolong.

HYMN 13.

1. Gently, Lord, O gently lead us,
   Thro' this lonely vale of tears;
Thro' the changes thou'st decreed us,
Till our last great change appears:
When temptation's darts assail us,
   When in devious paths we stray,
Let thy goodness never fail us,
   Lead us in thy perfect way.

2. In the hour of pain and anguish,
   In the hour when death draws
      near,
Suffer not our hearts to languish,
   Suffer not our souls to fear:
And, when mortal life is ended,
   Bid us on thy bosom rest;
Till, by angel bands attended,
   We awake among the blest.

HYMN 14.

1. Thanks to thee, our heavenly Father,
   For that kind protecting care,
Which has borne us on our pathway,
   And with blessings crown'd the
      year:

By thy kindness we have gathered
   Blossoms rich from learning's tree;
And for blessings ever grateful,
   We would yield our hearts to thee.

2. Ever in the future guide us,
   As we rove o'er life's dark sea;
And when sorrow's clouds encom-
      pass,
   May we steadfast trust in thee:
Thanks to thee, our heavenly Father,
   For that kind protecting care,
Which has borne us on our pathway,
   And with blessings crown'd the
      year.

HYMN 15.

Peace of God, which knows no meas-
      ure,
   Heavenly sunlight of the soul,
Peace beyond all earthly treasure,
   Come, and all our hearts control:
Come, almighty to deliver,
   Nought shall make us then afraid;
We will trust in thee forever,
   Thou, on whom our hope is stayed.

MODERATO

Un - to Him that loved us, and washed us from our

sins, and washed us from our sins in His own

blood, and hath made us kings and priests un - to God and His

Fa - ther; to Him be glo - ry and do - min - ion for-

ev - er and ev - er, for-ev - er and ev - er. A - men.

"Worthy is the Lamb."—ANTHEM.

Wor-thy is the lamb that was slain, To re-ceive pow-er, and

rich-es, and wis-dom, and strength, and hon-or, and glo-ry, and

bless-ing. Bless-ing, and hon-or, and glo-ry, and pow-er,

bless-ing, and hon-or, and glo-ry, and pow-er, be

un-to Him that sit-teth up-on the throne, and

"Worthy is the Lamb."—Concluded. 243

un - to the Lamb for - ev - er and ev - er. A - men.

"Thou wilt show me."—Anthem

Thou wilt show me the path of life. In Thy pres-ence is

ful-ness of joy, And at Thy right hand there are pleasures, there are

pleas-ures for ev - er ev - er more. Thou wilt show me the

path of life, Thou wilt show me the path of life.

I will lift up mine Eyes.—Sentence.

R. R. H.

I will lift up mine eyes to the hills, I will lift up mine eyes to the hills, I will lift up mine eyes to the hills, from whence com - eth my help; My help com-eth from the Lord, my help com - eth from the Lord, my help com - eth from the Lord, which made heav - en and earth.

Cast thy Burden on the Lord.—Anthem. G. F. R. 245

Cast thy bur - den on the Lord. And he will sus - tain thee:

Cast thy bur-den on the Lord, And he will sus-tain thee, And he will sus-

tain thee, and com-fort thee: He will com-fort thee, He will com-fort

thee: Cast thy bur - den up - on the Lord, Cast thy bur - den up-

on the Lord, and he will sus - tain thee and com - fort thee.

Thou wilt Keep Him.—ANTHEM. G. F. R.

Thou wilt keep him in per - fect peace whose mind is stay'd on Thee,

Thou wilt keep him, Thou wilt keep him, Thou wilt keep him in per - fect

peace whose mind is stay'd on Thee. Trust ye in the Lord for - ev-

er, Trust ye in the Lord for - ev - er, For in the Lord Je-

ho - vah is ev - er - last - ing strength, is ev - er - last - ing strength.

O, Sing unto the Lord.

TEACHER.

1. O sing unto the Lord a new song; sing unto the Lord | all | the | earth:
2. Sing unto the Lord, bless his name; show forth his salvation from | day | to | day:

RESPONSE. **TEACHER.**

Praise ye the Lord.
Praise ye the Lord. 3. Declare his glories among the heathen, his wonders a-

RESPONSE.

mong all | people: Praise ye the Lord in his ho ly tem - ple.

4. For the Lord is great, and greatly to be praised; he is to be feared a- | bove all | gods: } Praise ye the Lord.

5. For all the gods of the nations are idols; but the | Lord made the | heavens: } Praise ye the Lord.

6. Honor and majesty are before him; strength and beauty are | in his | sanctuary: } Praise ye the Lord in his holy temple.

7. Give unto the Lord, O ye kindreds of the people, give unto the Lord | glory and | strength: } Praise ye the Lord.

8. Give unto the Lord the glory due unto his name; bring an offering, and come in- | to his | courts: } Praise ye the Lord.

9. O, worship the Lord in the beauty of holiness; fear before him | all the | earth: } Praise ye the Lord in his holy temple.

10. Let the heavens rejoice, and let the | earth be | glad: Praise ye the Lord.

11. Let the sea roar, and the | fulness there- | of: Praise ye the Lord.

12. Let the field be joyful, and all that | is there- | in: Praise ye the Lord in his holy temple.

13. Then shall all the trees of the wood rejoice be- | fore the | Lord: } Praise ye the Lord.

14. For he cometh, for he cometh to | judge the | earth: Praise ye the Lord.

15. He shall judge the world with righteousness, and the | people with his | truth· } Praise ye the Lord in his holy temple.

O give Thanks unto the Lord.—Chant.

G. F. R.

1. O give thanks unto the ⎰
   Lord, for......... ⎱ he is good: For his | mer-cy is for- | ev-er.
3. O give thanks unto the | Lord of lords: For his | mer-cy is for- | ev-er.
5. To him that by wisdom | made the heav'ns: For his | mer-cy is for- | ev-er.
7. To him that........ | made great lights: For his | mer-cy is for- | ev-er.
9. The moon and stars to | rule by night: For his | mer-cy is for- | ev-er.

2. O give thanks unto the | God of gods: For his | mer-cy is for- | ev-er.
4. To him who alone.. | doeth great wonders: For his | mer-cy is for- | ev-er.
6. To him that stretched ⎰
   out the earth a-.... ⎱ bove the waters: For his | mer-cy is for- | ev-er.
8. The sun to......... | rule by day: For his | mer-cy is for- | ev-er.
10. O give thanks unto the ⎰
    Lord, for......... ⎱ he is good: For his | mer-cy is for- | ev-er.

Blessed is the Man.—Chant.

1. Blessed | is the | man
   That walketh not in the | counsel | of the un- | godly:

2. Nor standeth in the | way of | sinners,
   Nor sitteth in the | seat — | of the | scornful.

3. But his delight is in the | law of the | Lord,
And in his law doth he | meditate | day and | night.

4. And he shall be like a tree planted by the | rivers of | water,
That bringeth forth his | fruit — | in his | season.

5. His leaf also | shall not | wither,
And whatsoever he | doeth | shall — | prosper.

6. The ungodly | are not | so,
But are like chaff which the | wind — | driveth a- | way.

7. Therefore the ungodly shall not | stand in the | judgment,
Nor sinners in the congre- | gation | of the | righteous.

8. For the Lord knoweth the | way of the | righteous;
But the way of the un- | godly | shall — | perish.   Ps. i.

The Law of the Lord.—Chant.

1. The law of the Lord is perfect, con- | verting the | soul:
The testimony of the Lord is | sure, making | wise the | simple.

2. The precepts of the Lord are right, re- | joicing the | heart:
The commandment of the Lord is | pure, en- | lightening the | eyes

3. The fear of the Lord is clean, en- | during for- | ever:
The judgments of the Lord are true and | righteous | alto- | gether.

4. More to be desired are they than gold, yea than | much fine | gold:
Sweeter also than | honey, and the | honey- | comb.

5. Moreover, by them is thy | servant | warned:
In keeping | them is | great re- | ward.

6. Who can under- | stand his | errors?
Cleanse thou | me from | secret | faults.

7. Keep back thy servant also from pre- | sumptuous | sins;
Let them not have do- | minion | over | me.

8. Then shall I | be up- | right;
And I shall be inno- | cent from | great trans- | gresion.

9. Let the words of my mouth, and the meditation | of my | heart,
Be acceptable in thy sight, O Lord, my | Strength and | my Re- | deemer.

Ps. xix. 7—14.

250   The Lord is my Shepherd.—CHANT.

1. The Lord is my Shepherd, I | shall not | want:
   He maketh me to lie down in green pastures; he leadeth me be- | side the | still — | waters.

2. He restoreth my soul; he leadeth me in the paths of righteousness, for his | name's | sake.
   Yea, though I walk through the valley of the shadow of death, I will fear no evil; for thou art with me, thy rod and thy | staff, they | comfort | me.

3. Thou preparest a table before me in the presence of mine enemies; thou annointest my head with oil, my | cup runneth | over.
   Surely goodness and mercy shall follow me all the days of my life, and I shall dwell in the | house of the | Lord for- | ever.   Ps. xxiii.

God, be Merciful unto Us.—CHANT.

1. God be merciful unto | us, and | bless us,
   And cause his | face to | shine up- | on us.

2. That thy way may be | known upon | earth,
   Thy saving | health a- | mong all | nations.

3. Let the people | praise thee, O | God;
   Let | all the | people | praise thee.

4. O let the | nations be | glad,
   And | sing — | for — | joy:

5. For thou wilt judge the people | righteous- | ly,
   And govern the | nations up- | on — | earth.

6. Let the people | praise thee, O | God;
   Let | all the | people | praise thee.

7. Then shall the earth | yield her | increase;
   And God, even | our own | God, will | bless us.
8. God will | bless — | us:
   And all the ends of the | earth shall | fear — | him.　　　　Ps. lxvii.

O come, let us Sing.—CHANT.

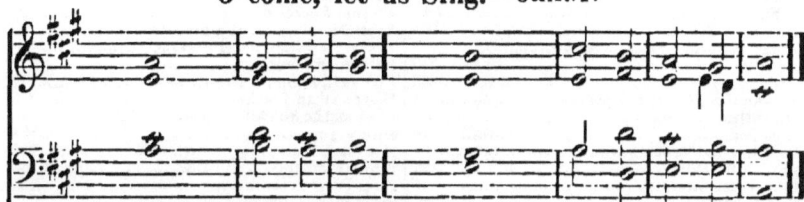

1. O come, let us sing un- | to the | Lord;
   Let us make a joyful noise to the | Rock of | our sal- | vation.
2. Let us come before his presence with | thanksgiv- | ing,
   And make a joyful | noise unto | him with | psalms.
3. For the Lord is a | great — | God,
   And a great | King a- | bove all | gods.
4. In his hand are the deep places | of the | earth;
   And the strength of the | hills is | his —- | also.
5. The sea is his, | | and he | made it;
   And his hands | formed the | dry — | land.
6. O come, let us worship | and bow | down,
   Let us kneel be- | fore the | Lord, our | Maker.
7. For | he is our | God,
   And we are the people of his pasture | and the | sheep of his | hand.
　　　　　　　　　　　　　　　　　　　　Ps. xcv. 1—7.

Make a Joyful Noise.—*May be sung to the above Chant.*

1. Make a joyful noise unto the Lord, | all ye | lands;
   Serve the Lord with gladness, come be- | fore his | presence with | singing.
2. Know ye that the Lord | he is | God:
   He hath made us, and not we ourselves; his people, and the | sheep — | of
   his | pasture.
3. Enter into his gates with thanksgiving, into his | courts with | praise;
   Be thankful unto | him, and | bless his | name.
4. For the Lord is good; his mercy is | ever- | lasting,
   And his truth en- | dureth to | all gener- | ations.　　　　Ps. c.

CONTENTS.

The signs prefixed to some of these titles indicate the authors of the words:

* M. B. C. Slade.   † Paulina.   ‡ Wm. O. Cushing.

Good Night.

Bethfessel.

MODERATO.

And now we say to all, Good night; And now we say to all, Good

night..

night; And now we say to all, Good night; And now we say to all, Good

night, good night, good night, good night, good night, good night, good night.

www.ingramcontent.com/pod-product-compliance
Lightning Source LLC
Chambersburg PA
CBHW030358270326
41926CB00009B/1160